FROM HELL TO HERE

This is the true story of an alcoholic's life, from early addiction, through its influence, to final release. However, all names have been changed, with the exception of "Mom" Turpin and Gwen Bull.

FROM HELL TO HERE

By

BONNIE PATTERSON

THE CHRISTOPHER PUBLISHING HOUSE
BOSTON, U.S.A.

THIS BOOK IS DEDICATED TO

ALCOHOLICS ANONYMOUS

The association which from coast to coast helped pave my road to sobriety and a new life; to its active sincerity and dedication to cause;

The innumerable doctors, nurses and counsellors by whom my progress was aided;

My beloved husband, ever near and understanding.

TABLE OF CONTENTS

REMEMBER TO PRAY

My road was rough, tragic and long;
No turning in sight.
All hope was gone.
I traveled this road by night and by day;
I'd even forgotten just how to pray.

Now, you don't have to go to the end of the road,
Just talk to the Master;
He'll carry your load.

Turn back, my friend, and start back today.
You'll make it for sure —
Just remember to pray.

All will be glory as you start life anew;
Nothing but happiness in store for you.
Your soul filled with sunshine, glory and bliss
Then you'll know just what you have missed.

Keep on, keeping on — day after day.
Just remember one thing:
Don't forget how to pray.

This poem is dedicated to "Mom" Turpin, who befriended and
encouraged me for so many years.

ACKNOWLEDGMENT

Grateful acknowledgment of help and advice in the planning of this book is made to Doris McGill Watt who gave invaluable assistance in the preparation of the manuscript; and to "Mom" Turpin, without whom this autobiography may never have been inspired.

PREFACE

In introducing this book, may I state that it is with sincere honesty that I relate facts and incidents. I was very much present in each of the incidents, and many of the people and places described in my story have survived the years. Anonymity is, of course, to be expected.

It is my sincere prayer that the story will help someone — someone who may be headed down the long, tragic road of alcoholism as I was not too many years ago; or someone who is attempting a recovery, as I, too, have experienced. If the reader is a beginning drinker, or "social partaker", take note of just what can happen, and did happen to me, along the wrong course. Be consoled, if an excessive drinker on the verge of acute alcoholism, that it is never too late to turn away and change the course.

I owe my life and much more to a wonderful club and the members within that association. In that society there are arms of welcome awaiting you; by name this sympathetic organization is called Alcoholics Anonymous. As a member of this marvelous association one has no obligation of monetary dues or fees, just the sincere desire to stay sober. There are no graduation exercises as such; but there are many helpful programs applying human sympathy and self-discipline for their utmost benefit.

If you are in doubt as to the purposes and ideals of

the Alcoholics Anonymous Club, as I was for such a long time, give my friends a try. Go to an "A.A." meeting and heed the voices of bitter experience. Just keep going, on and on, and if truly sincere, you are bound to find a better, richer way of life.

I

EARLY TIMES

This book possibly will seem to be an exaggerated testimonial to some of its readers, as it is composed of daydreams interwoven with nightmares; broken and shattered dreams that in time were miraculously changed into a beautiful dawning in my life.

As I reminisce over the past forty years, I too would think it a freakish, incredibly foolish story — had I not been present myself. It seems almost impossible to account for that ultimately beautiful dawning from that desperate, dismal darkness in which my plight begins. But as deepest darkness always precedes dawn, my story emerges happily — its ending being the answer to a sincere prayer.

After many wasted years of confusion, drinking much to excess, and the resulting jails, hospitals, sanatoriums, state institutions, psycho-wards, and therapy, there must be many incidents that I can't recall — many of which I may be happier not ever recalling. Due to acute alcoholism that had no temporary relief, shadowing a future life either with or without addiction, I was a dying, hopeless, helpless human waste until I completely surrendered my life to God. On many attempts it seemed a thing quite impossible for me to do.

The settling dusk and the creeping dawn of revelation sometimes don't seem real to me; it is only a long dream, fluctuating between both extremes. I remember well, of course, that my life began weaving itself into a tangle while, on the surface, all early indications pointed to an average childhood, for I had many friends with whom to share the weekly routine of school, work and play.

The oldest girl of five children, I was born in a suburb of one of the South's largest cities. My parents were average in most respects but above average in the zeal of life. Daddy was an adept tradesman, small in stature and proud of his heavy mustache, which was meticulously tucked under at the sides. He loved his family avidly, though in the course of their marriage, he and Mother had what must have been more-than-average conflicts. As a parent, however, he was always ready for a joyous wrestle or a bit of teasing with us children.

Mother was completely dedicated to raising her family, tediously minding the details of her household, and resolved to the demands of community activities that come with a large family. Fortunately for us all, she was a healthy, vigorous woman, not lacking in sympathy and understanding.

The week's route was mapped for church functions, in which we were all active. As it properly should be, religion and religious training were the center of our lives as children. I was especially devoted to my weekly piano and "expression" lessons. All this training was to have an ultimate and crucial bearing on my later life.

During my youth I longed to be a foreign missionary, and a Circuit Court Judge, one of the most respected, active and dedicated leaders in the community church in which I grew up, was an inspiration to me. He spent much of his valuable time with me, often discussing my fervent ambition for the future while at the same time counselling my parents during a period of marital strife. I must have endeared myself to him, as he asked to adopt me when I was thirteen.

I was often sent by my church to adjoining cities to participate in debates on the Bible, and though most of my opponents were adults, somehow I always won. I managed to make myself well heard, but I had to stand on an apple crate in order to be seen. With encouragement from the Judge, and coaching from my father, I was a capable Bible commentator.

I appreciated my dad's knowledge of the Bible, and I looked forward to his helping me as I often sat on the floor by an old-fashioned lamp while he spelled words for me and explained the Scriptures, all the while helping and encouraging me with my debates. I loved him very much — someone to adopt me, and regardless of the circumstances, was out of the question — though I felt deep affection for the Judge.

My church activities were so very important to me that I have saved a "Certificate of Honor" for having had nine years of perfect attendance during that period of my life. My devoted friend, the Judge, recalls our rewarding fellowship among his ninety-odd years of service to God and man.

On my return home early one evening when only in the eighth grade, Mother met me at the door, dressed in a gingham-check housecoat with her hair neatly pinned in that voluminous bun. She looked at me, revealing her tear-streaked face and swollen eyes, and said, "I don't guess your Dad will be coming back home to us any more. But I wonder if he realized that his two babies sold milk bottles for food tonight."

With my arms around her, Mother assumed her usual role of patience and consolation. I told her that I would quit school the next day and get a job. Strange as it may seem, I fully realized the seriousness of my new responsibility.

Though Mother seemed to understand the reasons for their separation she was reluctant to divulge the details to me. In view of my new status, I felt I was due an explanation, so I began an investigation on my own as to my father's whereabouts, only to find heartache and sorrow. Possibly not realizing the impact of his decision in seeking employment building and selling houses in an adjoining state, he told me that he felt sure the new arrangements would be better for the family, emotionally at least. He anticipated better wages in the new locale, so he promised to send money home regularly; but his financial assistance to his family was spasmodic, and after many periods of neglect, conditions at home went from bad to worse.

My parents never divorced, and during the ensuing fourteen years we children, and even Mother, looked forward to Dad's biannual visits at Thanksgiving and Christmas. Following a cheerful, friendly visit he would drive away in his big truck.

With family bonds finally completely shattered and with no hope for a reconciliation, dusk began falling into my life, bringing the darkness and despair that was to last for many years. How sad that at fourteen years of age, rips and tears of family tragedy, heartaches and disappointments could wreck a girl's morale, rendering that young life void of its natural rights — useless until it could possibly be rewoven and replen-

ished with faith, hope and love and true happiness at
long last. The rejuvenation would be slow, but day
by day life grew more purposeful, and each day presented a personal challenge.

Remember the Big Depression in the Thirties, when
a dollar was mighty powerful, and when there was
just enough clothing and just enough food to sub-
sist on — even in more fortunate homes? It was
during those years, when I was fourteen, that my
parents separated, leaving me, the oldest girl in the
family, to think of the future of the younger ones. I
felt a tremendous responsibility, mixed with teen-age
confidence that I could tackle and conquer the world
if given half a chance. And yet at the same age of
innocence and naivete, I was also frustrated with
curiosity about the world and what the future held for
me. But I was eager to quit school and prove myself
helpful to my mother in her distress. As she felt she
should follow in my step, my sister Shirley, just a year
younger than I, decided to quit school and look for a
job with me.

Shirley and I knew we had to look our very best
while applying for our first position. Our own wardrobe was sparse, but thanks to our kindly neighbor
across the street, we fell heirs to many of her discards,
which fortunately fit us perfectly. We had always
admired Mrs. Smith's clothes, but we were partial
to a certain hat that she eventually gave us. We
always argued as to whose turn it was to wear it, but
on this momentous job-hunting day, we compromised,
and Shirley wore it.

We must have been a memorable sight as we, hand
in hand, boarded the street car for the eight-mile trip
into town: Shirley, in that tremendous, bowl-shaped,

vibrant orange hat, with a matching ribbon sash around her gingham dress; and I, blossoming in be-ribboned splendor — with matching socks.

Yes, we got a job that day, in a little drugstore where we were to assemble boxes back in the store-room. Through the door we could see the soda fountain in the front of the store. After working a few hours, Shirley suddenly started crying. I asked why.

She sniffled her answer, "Sister, let's go home. I see people gambling out there in the front."

I was shocked, as I had thought this to be a nice-looking drugstore. With tear-filled eyes we told the druggist that we were going home as we didn't like gambling, and that we had seen some of his customers gambling. The puzzled man handed us three dollars for our pay, and we fled straight to the car stop.

Alighting from the street car and running the several remaining blocks to reach home with our explanation to Mother, we found her in complete sympathy. She emphasized that she, too, didn't like gambling. And it was years until I learned how to match nickels for a coke!

The three one dollar bills were a welcomed sight to Mother, for the kerosene for the stove was nearly gone and the grocery supply was nil. Dad hadn't sent any money in several weeks, and we were in desperate need. The living room furniture had long been reclaimed for default in payment; but furniture was the least of our needs.

My oldest brother, whom I had nicknamed Red when he was young, was a fine specimen of a boy, very robust and athletic. He found a paper route in order to do his part in helping to keep the bean sack filled. We were a diligent trio, but even so the going was rough.

Shirley soon found a part-time job that paid considerably well for her age and lack of experience. As she was an energetic, blue-eyed blonde, it was evident that she would soon be a successful career girl.

I succeeded in finding a full-time job as a clerk in the basement of one of the city's largest department stores. I dressed in borrowed or donated clothes and got by on as few essential commodities as possible, and denied myself every single "extra" that may have made for a brighter appearance and outlook.

While literally struggling to and from work, I often wondered how many men left their families; and how that my own father, whom I had trusted so, could have failed me. I couldn't understand his motive, and pondering this unhappy situation repeatedly, I became a defeated cynic. Having lost all respect for the male gender, I wanted no association whatever with them. With circumstances so unnatural, day by day my life grew more empty and drab. Sharing that heavy responsibility and experiencing the burdens of adulthood too early soon took its toll, for in plotting the course of my future years I failed miserably. I missed the love and security that I had once known, and I became the most confused, lonely and bitter member of the family.

My department store job paid $7.50 per week, and it was a thrill for me to catch a "Dollar Day" in the basement. Payday was frustrating, for I had to choose whether to take home a few clothes for the younger children, or withhold that purchase in order to put a little more on the grocery shelf. It was always rewarding to return home and find little five-year old Buck with his big ice-blue eyes and blond ringlets to his waist, and seven-year old Polly, a wistful brunette, waiting on the porch step for me. As often as I could, I managed a special little surprise for them, as they were so very young and adorable. But it took every penny we three could muster barely to skim the surface of providing our basic necessities.

Weeks turned into months, and those long months added up to years, during which Dad's rare visits were interspersed with reciprocal ones from me. Going to his apartment to inquire of his health and circumstances, and ultimately to plead for his return to us, I always returned home without the news we longed for. Except for the fact that I enjoyed being with him for awhile, the trips were always in vain.

I began to smoke cigarettes as they seemed to soothe my nerves after a busy day at the store, but I always hid or abstained when my dad came to visit, as I knew he wouldn't approve. Knowing he would think it a disgraceful thing for his daughter to do, I never allowed him to see me smoke, though I thought he lived by a mysterious code of ethics.

After seven years of our pooling and pinching pennies, Polly and Buck were ready to finish grammar school, and managing for school expenses had really only begun. Red was making quite a name for himself in town and the surrounding communities pitching baseball, and quite often the whole family would watch his games, taking a lot of pride in his skill. After I had asked many, many times for the reason he always kept a lip full of tobacco, he finally told me that it made him pitch better. He became such a good pitcher that the great day soon came when he was called to pitch in the major leagues. At least he was commanding what was to us a stupendous salary for the two and a half years that he was throwing his arm away. He returned home in time to attend Buck's and Polly's graduation exercises, all of which seemed a glorious climax to a long campaign.

In the meantime I had been waging a battle for self-importance, and with the emotional and physical strain of the years, I had become more bewildered and confused, even irrational. Perhaps it was here that the seed of that poisonous plant, Alcoholism, was sown. Liquor had never been allowed in our home, but having been out in the business world and left somewhat to my own devices, it didn't take me long to discover the "magic" of it, and where it could be bought "bootleg". It was called "white lightning", but by any name, proof, or source, it softened the burden of realism.

I was twenty-two when I decided to get married, culminating a puppy love courtship from my earliest teens during golden school days. When he had come to see me I nearly folded with embarrassment, as often we had no chairs to sit on, since first one furniture company and then another had come to repossess their merchandise, usually after thirty days. In retrospect, there was almost a comical cycle of furniture delivery and reclaim, but the financial circumstances were far from amusing. But now that Buck and Polly were past their crucial schooling, living conditions were much improved and showed hope for a much brighter future for Mother, even though she was still a lonely, heartbroken woman, aged beyond her years. I thought that I could start feathering my own nest then; but sadly, something was to happen to the feathers.

My husband and I lived in small apartments, which

were always garnished with liquor bottles left lying askew from our constant parties — night and day, week-end after week-end. Our quarters, though small, accomodated many a guest who "passed out" and spent the night where floor space was available. I was flying high with all our entertaining, fascinated by the usual party antics, but standing by to cook for our guests — in case they were able to eat the following morning.

In consenting to marriage, I managed to convince my husband that I should continue working to aid in the support of Mother and to help send Buck to college, and to do as much as we could for Polly in furthering her education. Buck worked while studying, and with some assistance, he eventually became a lawyer; but Polly compromised by taking a business course downtown. I enjoyed domestic security, financially speaking at least, as my husband was a successful automobile salesman, enabling me to spend my own salary as I chose. My choice of purchases was a steady supply of liquor, and with the relaxed economic strain, I acquired a status symbol for the times by choosing the real bonded brands of whiskey, though I knew from experience that "white lightning" afforded the same result.

The old resentment of and bitterness toward men rekindled itself as our marriage became a farce, and I began to shrink with constant misapprehension and discontent. Pitifully realizing that my mixed emotions and dissatisfaction could have been borne out of a troubled period in my youth, I was hoping to overcome some of the emotional discomfort and build up fortitude, and overcome all my problems rationally. Seeking new foundations on which to restore an unhappy marriage, I was to find that Mr. Booze provided no lasting support. Despite all the pitfalls, I depended on drinking parties to make my personal life more bearable — even happy and gay on a veritable merry-go-round. I was no longer available to cook or help with the "hang-overs" — I really led the party and became a fullfledged "booze-hound" hostess to compete with the most inebriated guest.

Meanwhile, as I coped with inner conflicts from all sides, Shirley decided to take the big step and got married. As she left Mother's for her new home, her path nearly crossed with Red's, as he was returning home, married to a wonderful girl whom the family always credited with having been responsible for his success in business. It saddened us to learn that our handsome sportsman had been stricken with an incurable heart disease. Despite the various transitions, the five of us having reached adulthood at last was somewhat of a relief in many respects, though I little realized the dismay in my own future.

At this period, I didn't realize, either, that my excessive drinking was a latent disease; I knew only that alcoholic beverages lent to my life the idealism I sought. Shirley soon found that her marriage could not be successful, and soon sought a divorce; and inasmuch as my own husband was a generous drinker, I, too, became inconsiderate, without accepting any blame for my own stormy marriage.

Hoping that conditions would be better and tensions relieved upon my return, I thought that the Chicago World's Fair offered an excellent opportunity to get away for a change of scenery. This was to be the first of many such decisions, as I often deemed it advisable to look for greener pastures, which were ultimately to lure me far from my native surroundings. With a little self-analysis, I knew I had a lot to learn, but I secretly yearned to transform myself from my unpolished status to a debonair sophisticate. Agreeing that sometimes "absence makes the heart grow fonder," we discussed the possibility of my taking a vacation. As we both were working and had accumulated a nice savings account, there was little reason why I couldn't continue my plans. Taking my first really long trip, I boarded the northbound train with three girl friends, anticipating an exciting vacation.

For the first time in my life, and I had been to many a party, I had my fill of what I called "ready-made" cocktails. I splurged and tried all the specialties at the magnificent Sherman Hotel, where, at the time, Phil Harris' band was performing. Wearing my first evening gown, I felt as if I were a princess in another world, captivating in appearance, but captured by my alcoholic dreaming. With the soft lights and music there, and the fabulous events at the Fair, the lavish vacation I afforded myself was a memorable occasion in my life. I was getting a new lease on life, but the week of holiday atmosphere was not enough.

Returning home with renewed hope for a compatible marriage, I endeavored to do special things to enliven the spirit of our relations, but somehow my attempts went awry more often than they were successful. Within a few months we were back to the old maladjusted pattern of discontent. I was a mystery even to myself, and an easy victim of alcoholism.

One Sunday when we had all gathered for a visit with Mother, I remember Shirley announcing, while we girls were primping at Mother's antique mirror in her bedroom, "I'm going so far that it will take ten dollars to send me a post card."

I thought it terrible for her to make such distant plans, but the idea appealed to me also. Although I understood her anxiety about the opportunity to make a fresh start after her own disappointment in marriage, I lamented that I was supposed to be a dutiful married woman and was expected to stay home. But as she left to sail for Hawaii on her new government job, my feet felt an urge to wander. My thoughts wandered, too, as I recollected our early childhood of playing little-girl games and sharing the difficult years that followed, and I knew that I would miss her. As the months of dissatisfaction mounted, I consumed more and more alcohol, seeking a respite from myself and my empty environment.

II

HITTING THE ROAD

My youthful ambitions to be a missionary in the field were now completely reversed. I wanted to gain personal importance and sophistication above all, and I featured myself thus, though I was self-deceiving in my methods. Thanks to downing all the whiskey I could get my hands on, I was satisfied with the image I saw in the mirror. Looking through rose-colored glasses, I seemed to have everything — finesse, security, and a husband with whom I may have had some disappointments, but I was secure in the knowledge that he was at least faithful to me. I remember thinking that should he ever prove unfaithful to me, however, I was attractive enough (and certainly clever enough) to cast him aside and do much better in another choice for myself.

I gathered a new circle of drinking friends in the dress shop where I had been working for nearly three years since my resignation from the department store. In fact, my husband and I didn't mingle with people who didn't drink, thinking that people who didn't indulge surely didn't know how to be sociable. I didn't see much future in worry or concern for anyone else's convictions, as I easily found solace in drinking away my problems.

Fortified by drinking constantly, I thought I could begin to restore my respect for men in general and my husband in particular. Boosted with additional "spirit,"

I found it possible to help some of my shop friends on various occasions with personal and financial favors, backed only by the little trust I so generously afforded them. What a shame that this new concentration of confidence, faith and liberality was falsely acquired with whiskey.

The day came, during my self-instructed course in benevolence, when I was told that one of my closest friends, to whom I had lent money, had for over a year deceived me. The news swept me completely off my feet. I had just been blind and too drunk to see our marriage finally disintegrating, and now that I feared it was true, I recognized my contributing faults. It was then, in 1940, that my world was darker than ever before, for all that artificial confidence was gone. Faith and love completely left my heart, broken and vulnerable — for remorse, hatred and misgivings to enter. I relied even more heavily upon drinking to help me forget the misery that had encompassed my life.

Even as my husband was trying repeatedly to make our marriage succeed, pleading for my forgiveness, we continued drinking heavily to dull our reasoning. During the next few days our relationship improved none, so I began to sort and pack ten years' accumulation, and to carry out a separation which ultimately led to a divorce.

During this period of my own personal tribulation, Pearl Harbor was attacked, and the gloomy day following my husband enlisted in the Armed Services and I returned to live with Mother. I really needed to escape at this instant, but whether by choice or predicament, I stayed with Mother for nearly a year, drinking day and night. Pretending to drink to get away from

myself was futile; I always found myself miserable.
A drink was imperative to get up on, to eat with, and
to go back to bed on; but I disproved it to myself to
some degree by saying that it was essential to escape
on. I still wanted to go somewhere and get away
from myself, but further than was possible by drinking. I sensed that though my family was wonderful
and sympathetic during my stay there, they seemed
concerned about something too. I wondered what was
bothering them.

I didn't have a job while I was staying with my
family, but I was cushioned by a savings account of
several hundred dollars left in my name following the
divorce. I managed to keep two liquor stores in
business for the next five or six months, during which
time it seemed that the operators would jubilantly
spot me coming a block away and have my choice
ready for me. One of the stores profitted mightily
during my five months as a steady customer, until I
actually became ashamed of myself for being there
from sun-up until midnight; to the point that I scolded
the proprietor for selling me liquor. I sobered somewhat when he looked at me, lowered his heavily
browed eyes and said, "It should be against the law
to sell you as *much* liquor as I do. But it's a free
country, and if you want to drink enough to kill a mule,
then I'm obliged to sell it to you."

After bombarding him with an angry retort, I took
my business to his major competitor next door, which
I felt would do untold damage to his profits, as revenge
for his comment. At my going rate in those days, it
probably did cause a depression in his income.

The time I spent in bars was almost forced upon me
because my family, except for Red who was especially

sympathetic with me and my misfortunes, would pour whiskey down the drain and throw the bottle out the back door as fast (it seemed faster) as I could bring it home. Red would rather absorb the product than waste it, and before long we were both drinking three meals a day.

But the day came too soon when Red realized that his excessive drinking was taxing his already precarious state of health, and whether on conviction or necessity he united with the rest of the family, who were thoroughly sickened by my addiction. Thus it occurred to me to take tactical action and hide the bottles in the shrubbery out in the front yard. With good timing I could manage a drink or two undetected by the working members of the family as they passed within inches of my cache on departure and return. However, when Autumn rolled around that year, my good hiding places were revealed. The gathering of fallen leaves divulged a residue of "dead soldiers" that would put a popular roadhouse in the shade. (I wonder if anyone ever looked up in the attic?)

Come hell or high water, I was determined to get my drinks, and when I could no longer persuade Red to get me a bottle or wasn't sober enough to get to a source myself, I could always rely on a particular cab driver to answer my call, and have it delivered to the door. The aging little man often responded to Mother's own call when she ultimately had pity on me as I pleaded in agony to her compassionate nature. To add to the family's exasperation, money was near total depletion, and I resorted to my first encounter with white wine. Even though it was much cheaper than whiskey, I could "step high" and reach my goal just by consuming enough.

I shall never forget the horrifying night that delirium tremens occurred from excessive white wine. Stretched convulsively on Mother's living room sofa, I cuddled and cooed to the little baby I saw on the pillow propped by my side. With all the family hovering over me in much distress, they insisted I stop all that foolish imagination about that "baby", but while I tried to convince them there really was a baby there, a doctor had been summoned. As none of them had ever witnessed such an attack, my family feared that I had reached insanity, but the doctor ended my hallucinations with paraldehyde. Naturally, my anxious mother stayed within arm's reach until dawn and recovery.

That first experience with delirium tremens had nearly mortified my family and me, and Red was so impressed that he, reportedly, never even took the top off another bottle. But despite that personal undergoing, I recovered only to anticipate more of my liquid satisfaction.

The frustration of trying to keep myself supplied with whiskey, especially after Red's "swearing off", amounted to near hate for all my family. Not a one of them was my ally. Mother even refused consolation, for she, too, feared another fitful attack; and it seemed that the maid would deliberately bump and expose my half-empty bottle hidden in the hems of the draperies as she used the vacuum cleaner. I had no hope for the future, no friends whom I could trust, no confidence in myself, and now my own family was abusing me by ignoring my needs. I decided I didn't have a chance of happiness there among cruel enemies, and that I must escape. Ironically, I sensed that I was fighting a losing battle.

Pondering my miserable family relationship and wondering how I could most effectively inflict some act of revenge, I decided early one morning to leave unexpectedly and pay my dad a surprise visit and tell him about the hateful treatment I was getting at home. After all, I hadn't done anything to any of them and they had all turned on me unmercifully.

Those were my thoughts as I started walking toward the little business section of our town via the muddy road from home. With a few drinks in me and a few remaining in the pint bottle that I had camouflaged with a rolled-up magazine, I headed toward the main highway, which was paved, and spotted the sole traffic light at the main intersection.

This is my lucky day, I thought as I reached the traffic light, for there I saw a neatly dressed gentleman driving a brand new automobile. Now's my chance, I thought, confident that I, too, was attractively dressed in my best, a navy blue suit with contrasting red shoes and hat; and I felt sure this man would be happy to have me as company.

Walking purposefully up to his car as if he had intended to meet me there, I asked him how far he was going. Looking me over, he answered, with natural surprise, "I'm only going about seventy miles," but I was in a hurry to get in that car no matter how far its destination, as the druggist on the corner was not only nosey but also a very close friend of the family. As the gentleman leaned over and opened the right front door, I lost no time in stepping inside, hoping that red light would soon change to green. Ours was a typical small town where your business was everybody's, and I had to be extra careful not to be seen getting in that car. Finally the green light flashed "Go"; what a relief it was to get away from that drugstore corner!

Perhaps the man was recuperating from this shocking experience, for he drove slowly for the next few blocks before asking, "How far are you going?"

He was obviously very puzzled about my sudden intrusion, though I knew he couldn't be very embarrassed by my presence, as I was nobody to be ashamed of. I returned his quizzical look and wondered if he had caught a "whiff" of my breath. He would have had good reason for his bewildered behavior, as ladies just didn't do as I did back in those days. Certainly they didn't invite themselves for a ride, particularly with a road stranger.

I told him that my dad lived not far from the place he was going and of my plan to get another ride on to my dad's. A bit hesitant at first to go into details about why I was going and why I had resorted to hitching a ride, I nonetheless replied in near truths to his numerous questions. When he asked why I was drinking, I felt I had no secrets left, but I didn't answer.

Knowing that he had already smelled liquor on me, I asked him if he minded my taking a drink in the car. He said, "I have no objection. It's your business, but I have no idea where to buy you one this early in the morning, Lady."

When I told him I had one with me an enlightened expression came to his face, and he slowed the car enough for me to retrieve my bottle from between the folds of the magazine, uncap the bottle and turn it up for my last drink.

It wasn't long until I could go into the details of

my life, answering all the why's and wherefore's he fired at me as we sped along the highway. I told him my name and he introduced himself, finally, so at least I wasn't revealing all my troubles to a complete stranger. I told him that I was going to live with my dad because the rest of the family was against me. They didn't understand anything I did or wanted to do, I explained, and they especially didn't understand why I took a drink occasionally. They even poured out all I brought home, I complained. He sat quietly as I rambled while we drove along.

Remembering a filling station ahead, with a very familiar place where whiskey was sold just behind it, I asked him to stop at the next station, as if for other purposes, and he obliged when it came into view. I anticipated getting lots done on this stop. I bought a bottle of "white lightning", called Mother to bid my family a fond farewell forever, and was on my way. Yes, I attended to all the chores as my chauffeur waited impatiently, drinking a coke.

As we continued the trip he informed me that he couldn't stop at another filling station because his time was limited. His family was expecting him and he only had two or three hours at home before his return to Atlanta. As we alternated with lengthy spurts of conversation, he seemed concerned about my visiting Dad in my condition, and as we approached the little town in which he lived, he stopped on the outskirts under a big oak tree and explained that he couldn't be seen in that "hick" town with a strange woman. He was well known around town, and that would never do. Discussing the situation further, he suggested dropping me by a little cafe ahead to wait for him to take me back where he found me. (I found him!)

I had already changed my mind anyway about surprising Dad, and I had called my family purposely to worry them. I got my "white lightning", so I had accomplished all I presently wanted and anything suited me.

As the car stopped at the little cafe, I thanked him for bringing me, and as I walked in the side entrance, promised I'd hang around until he came for me. I chose a back booth in order to have a few "Coffee Royales" while I waited for the next two hours. By ordering one cup of coffee, I planned to have many Royales in those two hours, as I knew how to stretch that one cup of coffee. I pretended to read the way-out-of-date magazine I'd brought with me as the waitress took my first and only order, though she offered many more cups of coffee. With one cup of coffee, my bottle and magazine, I entertained myself well until my ride reappeared tooting his automobile horn. Out I marched and I was just as surprised at his promptness as he was no doubt disappointed to find me waiting.

Realizing that I probably had emptied that bottle of liquor, he was apparently concerned, and on trying to figure some way to ditch me as we drove nearer to Atlanta, he suggested that he get me a new full bottle, call my family and talk to them himself; then take me back home where I belonged. His first suggestion suited me perfectly, but the other two were of little consequence. But I saw to it that his FIRST suggestion, my bottle, was carried out FIRST.

He lived up to his every word as he relayed my family's promise over the telephone that they would never pour my liquor out again. As I thanked him, he deposited me — bottle and all — at my mother's front doorsteps.

Alcohol was omnipotent; it held me with mysterious force, and I neither sought nor found any alternative.

Far away places beckoned as I considered my plight in 1942, so I advertised and sold all my worldly possessions, including leftover household furnishings, but my little old '36 coupe stayed in the family as I sold it to Red for ninety dollars. After juggling all my collateral, I had a little financial backing when I decided to pay a long overdue visit to my half brother — whom I hadn't seen in twenty years. My father had been a widower before he married my mother, but the children of his first marriage were by then young adults, and Pat had moved to California. The two families rarely corresponded, but we had recently received a letter from him. Prompted by the letter, though it certainly had issued no invitation, I departed for Los Angeles to start life anew out in the West. I breathed a sigh of relief as I boarded that Greyhound bus, bound for a long cross-country trip through wonderfully unfamiliar places. In planning my escape, I had packed two bottles of liquor in my suitcases, should my demand outlast the supply available, or should a congenial traveling companion appear. Except for the hold alcohol had on me, I was footloose and fancy-free.

All seemed fine and I was happy with my decision to relocate as we started off and progressed with the excursion, and intermittently I wondered what had caused all the bother and trouble with the family back home. I couldn't understand their lack of feeling — I had been treated unfairly; but the reason *why* was a mystery. What had I done?

Drinking merrily with a new-found friend, as anticipated, we soon found ourselves being invited off the bus in the middle of Texas by two very sober policemen. That late afternoon, as we were escorted some twenty miles across the beautiful prairie, the rolling tumbleweeds reminded me of my long hair, tousled by the speed of the automobile. On reaching the quaint little jail, I was separated from my long, lanky, typically Texan, traveling companion. I was to face a "drunk" charge, and I supposed he would be booked the same. However, I was quite surprised to learn that he was booked for what is known as a "paper hanger", having written bad checks in several states.

After the booking and being bedded down in jail to sober up, I couldn't help but wonder why I was being treated so shabbily here in this "Great State of Texas" where I thought good liquor and a good time were supposed to be commonplace. I had heard that whiskey was sold on nearly every corner, but evidently one was not supposed to drink it. I wondered why an innocent stranger like me, who was just passing through on a bus, should have to go to jail for being a "Roman".

It wasn't long until I had a change of mind and heart in my opinion of Texas, for the sheriff asked me in a bashful tone, if I'd like to join everybody in the little kitchen for a bite to eat. Though not hungry at all (but indeed, "thirsty") I accepted. Curious as to what was served for meals in a jail anyway, I found myself enjoying a nourishing home-cooked meal, much more tasty than I had thought the tiny two-burner wood stove capable of accomplishing.

Except for the barred windows, there was an atmosphere of what I imagined a mountain retreat, with the coffee aroma, rough though cozy furnishings, long-horns spanning the wall over the cabinet, and mounted trophies of several animals staring out of glassy eyes down at me. I was perhaps the only female ever to have been in that jail, but the novelty of the event was mutual. Though it was my first jail experience, I was to see many a monstrous police desk similar to the one that overpowered the otherwise pleasant surroundings of the little jail.

If you've never been in Texas, and especially in a small town there, where hospitality overflows, friendliness abounds, wine and other liquors flow freely, you don't know what you've missed — even in jail. I ate, drank and enjoyed Texas hillbilly music during the evening. But just like old times, however, I was asked to be the cook for the whole crew.

The jail crew would long remember the farewell breakfast that I was invited to cook before my departure. I fixed eggs for them all, and as do frog legs, the eggs kept hopping out of the pan. Anyway, they were promptly eaten, and however indigestible they proved to be, I never knew, for my police escort arrived to take me the twenty miles back for connections with the bus to continue my journey West. All in all, it had been a pleasant confinement, but I regretted to learn, in the meantime, that the sheriff was told not to report back to his duties the next day, having been charged with drinking on the job. (I hoped that the kindly gentleman host would soon find another position.)

I had heard that in Los Angeles, also, liquor could be bought by the barrel, and that sounded great to me as I anticipated my arrival. I imagined myself going into the nearest corner grocery store, buying all I wanted, and not hiding from anyone to drink it! On arriving at the scene of these green pastures, I was to find, within a few blinks of my Southern eye, that credit wasn't hard to get, either. In case I ran out of money (as I was sure to do), that problem was to be easily solved.

I had decided several days previously to wire my half brother, Pat, of my intended visit. Due to the layover in Texas, however, I was running two days behind scheduled arrival. He, in the meantime, had started out to meet my bus along the highway. Finally, after much waiting on one another, we arrived at his home, where four beautiful little girls greeted their long-lost aunt whom they had been anxiously waiting to see.

Pat had changed quite a bit during the years, but he resembled our father very much; being short, half-bald, and jovial. The little daughters were each captivating: Jane, just a year old and a tiny blue-eyed blonde; Penny, with a winning personality like her daddy's, was a perk three-year old with long blonde hair to contrast her big brown eyes; five-year old Dottie was a typical brunette and rather bashful; and Ruth, blonde though boyish, commanded a lot of responsibility for her seven years, as she proved her little self dependable in helping her busy mother. Diminutive Pauline was the lucky mother of these little dolls, and though they compensated for her multitude of daily household chores, I was puzzled by her look of dismay when first I saw her. Although she was a very attractive, congenial woman, lucky to have so many blessings, Pauline seemed mysteriously unhappy.

While sitting at the dinner table, later in the evening, Pat interrupted my quiet admiration for this family by saying:

"Sis, I take a drink occasionally, so don't you pay

any attention to it. I'm sure you don't fool with this stuff," he continued as he poured himself a generous glassful; "so don't you let it bother you, even though it was certainly taboo at home."

My attention was glued to that bottle he had set on the dining room table, and my intention was to empty it as soon as he retired for the night; and I did that very thing. The next morning, after accusing his wife (who had never taken a taste in her life) of drinking his liquor on the sly, and after her subsequent denial, he decided that perhaps the little ones had poured it out while playing, never knowing that it was *I* who had emptied it.

Pat was then currently laid off by his employer for excessive drinking, though the explanations had been withheld for the first day or so of my visit. Considering their financial status, I found that I couldn't depend on Pat to advance me any money, or to treat me to any of his beverage already on hand. It hadn't taken me long to run out of money, the way I spent it, so it was imperative that I find myself a job.

My luggage had been lost somewhere between Texas and Los Angeles and with my supply of clothes in a distressing state, I couldn't be choosy about where I worked. Accepting a job in a new laundry nearby, where all the women wore slacks, I solved that age-old problem of "what to wear". A pair of slacks and a shirt remained my sole possessions for weeks to follow.

After three months of checking out shirts and family laundry, I met the gentleman who had a share as second partner in the business. Shortly thereafter, I accepted his invitation to have dinner at the Brown Derby, thinking that I was at last going to get somewhere. Dressed up in clothes borrowed from a neigh-

bor willing to oblige me, I was swathed in green to
match his Packard automobile. I was ready when
he arrived and he courteously helped me into his car.
He was quite a handsome gentleman, graying slightly
at the temples and immaculately dressed, and I knew
we were a most attractive couple. As we rode along,
he jokingly said:

"I'm sure Southern belles like you don't drink, so
I won't tempt you. But I enjoy keeping whiskey in the
car for my personal use, and for friends who happen
to want to join me."

After he pushed a little button, out came a miniature
bar, revealing itself to be completely equipped. I
marvelled at it, wondering who had invented that
ingenious appliance, then decided that the details
didn't matter — it was too wonderful to resist. I was
accustomed to larger glasses, but the small ones were
fascinating, and quite easily refilled.

We drank in and out of the car as we hit the high
spots of Hollywood (where I learned that "they" drank
as much as I'd heard). We returned in time to see the
last floor show for the night at the Brown Derby,
where Fibber McGee and Molly were appearing in
person. Trying to keep up with my date's drinks and
figuring out the purpose for all that silverware kept
me well occupied. Imagine, I thought, a drunk like
me in the Brown Derby; but, I was getting sophisti-
cated.

The next morning, with swollen feet, aching head
and still half full of booze, I went on to work. At
8:00 my date called me into his office and asked if
I needed a drink. I surely did. From under his desk
he retrieved a bottle, which he had labeled, "For
Snake Bites", a new expression to me at the time.

(The sophistication to which I had aspired was slowly developing!) At noon, we were called into the office of the other owner and asked to leave until we were sober.

Inevitably, it didn't take long to drink myself out of the very door through which I had entered.

Unaware of my disease, I grew more and more fearful; anxiety and anguish filled my wretched soul. I was afraid to go to sleep and dreaded waking up. I drank rain or shine, fog or smog, to ruin fourteen years in the lovely state of California. To my heart's content (and even to my soul's) I drank shamelessly. It was so convenient to pick up a bottle at the nearest store; no standing in a trance over the counter of a "State Store" to compare prices and brands displayed so temptingly on the shelves.

Drowning my troubles was far easier than taxing my mind and soul with reasoning.

My biggest competitor proved to be Pat, as he managed to drink all that I brought in — by some hook or crook. Having no job, I couldn't begin to keep us both supplied. I was doing well getting all I needed for myself. Resenting his selfishness, I decided that he was a real drunkard and that I would have to move away.

But I didn't move far away — just next door. I was close enough to see if he was still drinking and yet far enough away that he wouldn't be bothering me or my liquor. I was also close enough so that if I ran out, I could find where he thought he was hiding his bottle from me — under the house (well hidden from his wife, but not from me!). I, too, found lots of new hiding places at my new address. Inside, outside, under large rocks that lay beside the driveway, in the porch awning that had been drawn up for the season, here, there, everywhere, I eventually found a likely spot. I felt safe for awhile but it wasn't long before my shrewd half brother was finding my bottles again.

The new address hadn't helped my situation as much as I'd hoped, so I deemed it necessary to leave Los Angeles for good — never to return. A new territory was to be my usual answer and resort, where I could start life anew. But nomads need traveling expenses, and my folks were always good for one more "touch" — especially when I placed an emergency and "collect" telephone call notifying them of my urgent medical predicaments. So, with twenty-five dollars that my daddy sent on the pretext of my having pneumonia, I started out, walking. Rather than spend dollars for bus tickets, I usually saved them for a more satisfying use. Thumbing my way proved more convenient as well as practical for all concerned. This way, I didn't have to ask a bus driver to stop and wait for me to grab a bottle, and occasionally get left, being either too slow or too drunk to make it back to the bus. And the beautiful sights in northern California could better be appreciated when unhurried. Though the silvery, snow-capped mountains were to become so familiar, I never ceased to be awed as I gazed at their magnificence from the roadside.

I traveled "light", cumbered with only an overnight bag containing a powder puff, a lime, and a bottle of gin. I could be seen for a "country mile", clad in those chartreuse slacks shining like a cat's eyes, and I was confident of getting a ride from somebody — anybody, going anywhere; the direction rarely made a difference.

I was magnetized by all the bars as I proceeded to

nowhere in particular, visiting many fascinating ones during my tours. Bartenders became my best friends, for in them I usually found willing listeners. So attentive were they to my drawled tale of woe that they were eventually as drunk as I, not noticing that the nickels they planked down on the counter for me to play the juke box rarely got past my pocket. I had my future drinks to finance. Often a spellbound bartender literally gave me drinks to keep me talking; but more often than not, they were unaware of their generosities. I liked to say that I was a stranger in town, and I usually was for at least a few days, successfully buttonholing many barflies, combining my favorite sports, drinking and talking, into my particular brand of "con" artistry.

A certain bar in Bakersfield boasted a luxuriously carpeted floor and a magnificent mirror in which you could see yourself, that spanned the length of the bar. In that critical mirror, I was attempting to fix my hair. With the latest song hits playing softly in the background, I soon became quite familiar with the staff, as my new acquaintances and I greeted each of the three shifts, and bade the night crew farewell as they closed for a few hours.

Then came the time that I couldn't find my reflection in the mirror; but I did find myself in jail that evening, with no mirror, no carpets, and the clanging of iron doors and the rattling of keys being the only "music". The whiskey smells were familiar, but when mingled with the fumes of paraldehyde and bathroom odors the result was additionally nauseating. Frantic, I at last found what I imagined to be a mirror and I initiated a lively conversation with myself as a bad case of delirium tremens developed. In that state of madness I was carried by a police ambulance to the General Hospital.

Upon regaining consciousness at the hospital, I remembered nothing of the past eight hours, but was soon to learn that my meager clothing (my only outfit) had been lost during admission to the emergency room. There was nothing for me to wear on appearing before the judge (which was also "news" to me) except the hospital-issue gown of crude cotton. I must have been a sight that judge will never forget! I thought the halo of yellow flowers that the nurses had entwined in my long hair lent an angelic effect to my unusual public costume. After the police had explained my case, the judge seemed overwhelmed with sympathy for the situation, nearly ignoring the charge against me. He dismissed me, much to my relief, and I was delighted with his instructions that I should return to the hospital until my clothes could be recovered. As a "guest" of the hospital for the next nine days, I actually enjoyed working with and helping the nurses as allowed, not realizing that the recent experiences, though often to be repeated, would have some ultimate and fringe benefits. When my little bundle of clothes was located, I was dismissed — clean, well, and vibrant.

Just seventy-five miles and two hours later I arrived in a thriving little city, abundantly equipped with a new supply of bars, bartenders and gullible barflies. Through one of my new acquaintances from a mutually favored bar, I found a job; but through no fault of my own, it was short-lived. I became so adept at inserting the little flourescent gadgets that light up when a car approaches that my supervisor realized

that I, by outworking him two to one, was a threat to
his own job. I certainly had no intention of "rolling"
him, but he released me, anyway.

With a little honestly earned money, I hit the highway again, headed for nowhere in particular. The
first opportunity for a lift was headed for Nevada,
and I was soon to arrive in the gambling capital of
the West. Much to my surprise, I noticed that
people everywhere were shoveling snow from their
drives, warmly dressed for the season at hand. Just
a few hours earlier I had been comfortable in my
tropical attire, but after a very short while roaming
the streets, I was desperate for warm clothes and a
place to rest my travel-weary bones. It didn't take
long for the police to notice my usual condition and
unusual apparel, and I welcomed the accommodations
to which they conducted me — the warm city jail.

After spending ten days in jail, I decided to explore
the rest of the city. Full of excitement and booze, I
began to hit the bars and gambling houses along
Fremont Street. After only five hours freedom, I
found myself in the same old predicament — limber-
drunk and frozen stiff. I almost welcomed the invitation of the same officers to return to the same jail.
Though not intending to rush my tour, I had seen
quite a bit of the town in a short time, and didn't ob-
ject strenuously to returning to warm quarters for an
additional thirty days. The only problem I considered
was managing to arrange passage for a bottle through
those narrow spaces between bars. I turned on my
Southern charm as necessary, and melted many a
heart.

Upon release, I headed for Los Angeles again, grant-
ing that perhaps it might be a pretty fair city after all.

With that sober reasoning, I thought of Pat, his family, and their dependence on me. I was particularly curious to know if he was sober; and if so, how. Via foot and innumerable hitched rides, I arrived in Los Angeles at night.

Rather than irk Pat by awakening him from his deep sleep (though there was the likely possibility that he might be in jail rather than at home), I found myself a place to roost in an all-night theater near the bus station. I called this place home for the next few days and nights, not being in such a hurry to investigate Pat after all. Eating popcorn, washing it down with booze of any kind, I'd curl up and sleep until 5 a.m. Then the janitors arrived for cleaning up, and out all of us booze-hounds went with the empty bottles, popcorn sacks and assorted trash. How sorry I felt for all those poor souls with me, as we hurried around the corner on skidrow to get that morning pickup, only to start another wasted day.

There are many routes from the mountain top of life down to skidrow, but only one craggy path leading back up. Skidrow cast such a spell over me that I was to find it very difficult (seemingly impossible, at times) to regain the apex of a normal life. I pitied the drunkards and winos; they were people of all classes and descriptions. They tottered on the streets, loitered in bars and leaned behind doorways, holding out their shaky hands for a piece of money with which to get just one more drink. I shared what little I had as long as my money or bottle lasted; slow to realize that I, too, was a shameful drunkard.

Skidrow can be any place, actually; not just in the slum section of town, but even in the finest home. Some habitants have silk sheets to sleep on in their fine skidrow; most of my rooms had no sheets at all — just a place to pass out horizontally.

Having found my way to Pat's home after many detours since returning to Los Angeles, I learned that he had been picked up on the streets and was serving time in the county jail. His sentence was thirty days for this current public drunkenness charge. I felt obligated to find a job to help his family so that they might at least eat; but unreliable as I actually was, the few jobs I secured I also forfeited. I tried with all my heart to make financial ends meet, but on my meager earnings it was impossible to feed six people and pay the rent — after first purchasing my demanded supply of liquor.

After having a long talk with Pat upon his return home regarding his excessive drinking and neglect of of his family, we decided that perhaps my theory of changing territory might help him too. The rest of the family would profit by the move because the neighbors had become very unfriendly.

We watched the paper together for several days, hoping to find an advertisement in the employment section that included housing for the workers' families. Finally, we found an entry that seemed promising, and not too far from the Los Angeles area on one of the largest chicken processing ranches in that part of the country.

Rather than have Pat leave his family, I volunteered to hitchhike to the ranch and get more details from the owner of the firm. I left the next morning, allowing myself time for a detour to the bar around the corner. There, after a few drinks, I placed a "collect" call to Mother. She cried sympathetically when I told her of the pending surgery on my foot, though actually

I was suffering miserably with angry blisters. The bartender and I had become well acquainted during the last several months, so during the course of the long, long distance telephone call, it was agreed that Mother would wire him twenty-five dollars to reimburse him for his generous loan to me for my operation. Knowing my mother, I'm sure he was repaid, but he surely did take a gamble on my having no identification whatsoever. After getting the little Mexican, who downed every drink he could wrangle, to play another tune on his cocktail-glass xylophone, I hurried out with my cash, ready to continue with our job plans. Luck was with me that day, for my charmed thumb and I were on the job site within three or four hours.

After locating the plant manager, Mr. Holtz, I explained to him that my wayward brother couldn't hold a job, and as a result his family was destitute. He thought I was very considerate to come 3000 miles across-country, especially with our father ill back in the South and unable to assist them in getting affairs straightened out. The manager fell for the whole story, word for word, as they poured forth from a little saint with a Southern drawl. When he heard the plight of the four hungry little girls, he was indeed sympathetic, and after he showed me the cabin and assured me that meals for the family were included, he even advanced me fifteen dollars with which to get that little family on his premises as quickly as possible.

With the matter settled very much in our favor, I set out for Los Angeles again to tell the good news. Since we would be moving out early the next morning, we decided to bid all the neighbors farewell that night, with the addition of a fifth of whiskey making for a joyous occasion. I had had a fruitful day and

thoroughly enjoyed the celebration. The neighbors enjoyed the party, too, mostly because we were leaving,
but little did they know that we would be returning
at the end of the week.

One neighbor was so jubilant that he offered his
services and his truck to help us move. Had he
possessed a larger truck, we might not have resorted
to setting most of our belongings back inside the house
and locking it behind us. For us, that was a blessing
in disguise. With bag and baggage our troupe transferred to the little cabin on the chicken ranch and as
I had promised the owner, we were ready for our jobs
early Monday morning.

As our dear neighbor hadn't charged us for his services and use of his truck in helping us get to the
ranch, we had a little drinking money. Following a
few toasts to our new venture, we manned our assigned posts in the huge plant and began de-feathering
and cutting up chickens.

There were long sinks equipped with funnel-shaped
contraptions into which the chickens' heads were
forced for decapitation. For the next phase of processing, the chickens were placed over de-feathering
spouts where powerful suction greatly expedited an
otherwise tedious manual task. The de-feathering
post was given to Pat, and I was assigned to help cut
up the chickens further down the assembly line as
they came through a big drain into the sink. The
chickens that I cut up were barely recognizable, having
an unusual number of parts as the end result of my
efforts, which must have puzzled many a housewife.

Pat's assistant at his de-feathering post was his
whiskey, and with that disabling partner he soon found
himself way ahead of the Mexicans who were taking

off the heads at the funnels — so far ahead that several poor chickens got de-feathered before their turn. On seeing naked chickens running around, the foreman wondered what was going on, and lost no time in finding out.

Upon inspection of my department, the overseer hardly appreciated my efforts and directed one of the Mexican girls to show me the correct way to cut up a chicken — just one more time. With my next attempt, there were even more parts than previously, despite the additional instruction.

Mr. Holtz gave us each a stern reprimand and warned us of the one remaining chance he would allow us. It was understandable that he was losing money as well as patience.

We were still working on the fifth day though our liquor supply was getting low. The fifteen dollar advance with which to finance our move had gone a long way toward the supply, but didn't begin to meet the demand. However, at least the children were being fed regularly on fried, broiled, stewed and baked chicken.

Visiting day rolled around during our brief occupation, bringing many people into the plant to see the process of readying chickens for market. The plant was one of the most modern in the nation, capable of processing so many chickens per minute, etc.; and they were certainly processed through that day, breaking all records — defeathering, dead or alive.

Getting our week's pay, minus the fifteen dollar advance, and minus a penalty deducted as a loss to the company, we were dismissed. But with the children and all the baggage to move, a contribution was gladly accepted.

Rather than waste money on transportation, we decided to call our one sympathetic neighbor again to move us back home, and quickly. He didn't need any explanations. We returned home Saturday noon to find that we were out of groceries, so Pat, still wearing his de-feathering uniform and rubber boots, volunteered to get enough for the week-end at the store around the corner. After several hours of waiting, we telephoned the jail and confirmed our suspicion that he had visited the bar instead of the store. He didn't return from his shopping errand for ten days.

I remained close to home, alternately looking for liquor and a job. I had had enough of that chicken processing plant, and I felt sure the feelings were mutual.

Within a few days I lost a newly acquired job in a dress shop after the manager detected my drinking on the premises and leaving the empty bottles in the fitting room. The discharge coincided with an ad in the newspaper, to which I applied as an experienced "fur saleslady". The job appealed to me and though I really didn't know skunk from mink, I convinced the store manager that I could handle the job quite capably.

The assistant manager, a very attractive blue-eyed blonde, while teasing me for my Southern speech, proved helpful in teaching me the essentials in selling furs. We became close friends within a few days, and to her I confided my efforts in trying to support my brother's family and myself with my salary (being careful not to disclose my own method of survival, obtained through a charge account in Pat's name at the liquor store around the block). Since he and I were famous patrons and enjoyed a fair reputation for paying (eventually), keeping myself supplied was a simple matter, for the present.

Painting the scenery at the homefront far prettier than any artist's conception, I found my artistry outdone by my new friend's revelation of her own plight. Her picture seemed far sadder than mine as she told me of her "Daddy", as she affectionately called him. He was her reason for working, as he was dependent upon her in his old age, but her efforts to keep him sober and on his feet were in vain. Little did she know how much we had in common, in truth.

One day she said that she would like for me to meet her daddy, further suggesting that we quit our jobs with the furrier and move up to the lake to work. Deciding that working conditions would be better there, and that I could send money to my family from there as well, I agreed to quit and accept her plans. I was also anxious to meet her daddy, whom she had described so vividly, boasting that a new dam had been named for him.

After promising faithfully to send a little money each week to help while Pat looked for a new job, now that he had been released from jail again, I packed the few clothes I had, a pint of gin rescued from its dubious hiding place, and left to meet my friend. We each had a small bag under our arms, were similarly dressed in slacks, and had bandanas tied around our heads. We waited for the bus. She was not aware that her travel suggestion was so convenient for me, as I had only my usual traveling outfit anyway. She hadn't noticed that I had worn the same dress everyday at the shop, either. But I noticed the obvious brown paper sack under her arm, and she hastened to explain that she always took her daddy a treat when she went home to visit him, as it was in-convenient for him to get to town from their place in the lowlands due to his health.

Soon after our arrival at the lake, I discovered it wasn't the distance alone that anchored "Daddy Boulder Dam" — it was the shape he was in! He greeted us lazily from an unsightly old hammock outdoors, and one breath later he looked straight into his daughter's eyes and scolded her harshly for keeping him waiting exactly seven weeks for that bottle. It seemed to me he hadn't shaved once during that long anticipation.

The sight of that tar-paper shack was indeed a con-trast to what I had been led to expect. And old Daddy was, indeed, a contrast to the retired tycoon I anticipated meeting. Pondering the situation for a few days, I came to the conclusion that he had arrived there and remained for understandable reasons.

The back of the house consisted of one long room across the rear, furnished with rough wooden tables and benches where construction workers met for meals; and the other room was a maze of army cots encircling the enormous wood stove in the center. Ignoring all those beds inside, Daddy Boulder preferred his pre-carious hammock outside.

We found our larder completely void of liquor and food after a few days, and of course the latter item was of little importance; but it became urgent that we find at least some wine. In the meantime, a friendly but very bewhiskered man had stopped by for a few minutes' visit, offering to do whatever he could to make our vacation more enjoyable, as he was our nearest neighbor from a mile away through the wilderness. With his being an unlikely remedy for our craving, it was decided that I could purchase some wine some six or seven miles away in the other direction. Conditions being such that there was absolutely no traffic along those roads, thus rendering my thumb useless for this trip, I asked our neighbor to lend me his horse for a short while. Time alone healed many problems, I knew, and I expected that a long time indeed would be needed before I could be in walking condition again after straddling that ancient, bloated animal; but the mission had to be accomplished.

After visiting ten days with the lake folks, part of which I spent recuperating from saddle fever, I bade the girl and her father farewell. I now knew that they were not the socialites I had envisioned, and felt pangs of disappointment in my new friend, not realizing that I had deceived her and Pat's family, also. I had spent every cent on wine for the three of us, and no profitable occupation loomed in the immediate future. Had not Mother Nature redeemed the "vacation" with the splendor of her deep blue lake reflecting the towering mountains and riotous color rays of sunsets, I would have emerged completely the loser.

III

BYWAYS OF CALIFORNIA

The following ten months were spent on the highways of California, going further down the tragic route of acute alcoholism at the same time — in a nightmare of unawareness of my disease as much as anything else. I did decide that the climate was nicer in Nevada, and that good-paying jobs were readily available there. Considering how badly my relatives and I needed the money, I knew this to be a feasible decision, so I started thumbing my way in that direction. My decisions were sown shallow, easily washed away into oblivion, only to be repeated. I was traveling lighter — carrying only the bottle, and dressed comfortably in my chartreuse uniform. I no sooner arrived in Nevada, after many detours and delays, than I changed my plans.

It was Dad's turn to get that collect call for money, and I could always finagle a little more out of him. By alternating my appeals, they could build up a little reserve in my name, perhaps; and though Mother usually operated with a deficit, she never refused my urgent appeals. Western Union and I usually went around and around about my lack of identification or credentials when the money arrived, but another tale of woe was the solution.

With money in my pocket, I started hitch-hiking again, with a definite aim for Los Angeles at last. I did so purposely to see if Pat had reformed and was

supporting his family. Then, I thought, after his
promise to stay with his job, prove himself a man and
stop all the drinking, I could return to my original
and personal plans for Nevada. If he kept his promise,
I'm sure he stayed sober, for it took four months for
me to return and investigate.

Due to that recent case of pneumonia for which my
father had sent me thirty-five dollars, I felt richer than
I had in many months, but neither feelings or money
lasted long at the bar in Nevada. I was entertaining
all the other barflies with my Southern drawl, and
drinking all the booze anyone would buy me to keep
up the chatter. The music and bright lights furnished
a new fascination and as that tremendous bar loaded
with coins in all denominations revolved, I was literally hypnotized. I clawed madly to pick up a few
pieces of that cargo with which to buy drinks for the
next day, until finally I became so numbed that I
could hardly see or feel the heavy plate glass that
was holding all that money securely beneath. The
proverbial "loose money" there was well guarded after
all. As my condition became worse, I began to wonder
if I were losing my mind, going off my rocker, or just
what was causing the new sensation I was feeling. As
usually did happen, it seems, I landed in the county
jail, and the revolving bar remained vivid in my memory, though I no longer desired to be under its spell.
I was peculiarly sick.

Two policemen conducted me to the jail to spend
the next five days sobering up, but at the onset of
delirium tremens I was transferred to the General
Hospital to remain for twelve days of treatment.

Restrained by cuffs on my hands and feet so I
could not butt my brains out (if I had any left), I lay

torn between the real and the unreal, subconsciously wondering if all that money I'd seen in the bar was real. A few hours later when the attack subsided and as the nurses combed and braided my tousled hair, tidied things up for the meal, I appreciated their goodness and sympathy, and wondered why I couldn't command my life into a worthy course.

Realizing the seriousness of my condition, I attempted to question one of the doctors about my health and circumstances. I didn't remember being arrested, or being admitted to the hospital. The most vivid thing in my memory was the money at the bar, so I asked him why it was there, and why I wanted to pick it up. Looking at me intensely, he said, "All the money in Nevada wouldn't help you, I'm afraid. The help you need can be self-administered and wouldn't cost a red cent." That was a devastating statement to hear, and one that I didn't understand. What had happened to me; or what had I done? Scared to death with the general atmosphere of things, I was afraid to ask further questions.

I told the hospital administrator a week later that I had to get to Los Angeles to inquire of my family there. Explaining that Pat was a hopeless drunkard neglecting his family, I emphasized how desperately they depended on me for financial help and moral support.

"What kind of help do you think you are capable of giving?", he asked. "If you can't help yourself with your own personal problems, then you can't be of any great assistance to him." This deduction of his didn't register with me at all — my mind was so warped that I didn't know what he meant. I knew I could help myself — to liquor; and that I still wanted to help myself to that shining money under the bar glass. The administrator's advice was futile, wasted on incomprehensive ears.

With the doctor's release, I was a free gal again, ready to return to the highways after squandering the remainder of the money which my father had wired for the hospital bill. I liked the way the local clubs stayed open from dusk 'til dawn, and I wanted to get back to my beat.

I hung around in the throngs that crowded the streets, following the drift toward the slot machines that were highlights of the area. I was as much captivated by them as by the bars, frustrated as to where I could best spend my few coins. Once in a while if I hung around certain people they'd hand me a handful of coins to try my luck, fascinated by those temperamental machines, pleading with them to break for me. I was badly in need of money in a place where I saw more of it than ever before or since.

Choosing another exclusive club, purposely avoiding the one with the revolving bar, I sauntered around hoping to find someone with whom to perch on a bar stool. My exploring led to the second floor, to which I tried to ride my first escalator, and if the alert gentleman behind me hadn't caught my sprawling form, I wouldn't be here today to write my story! After that sobering experience, I found a telephone booth and called Mother for some money. I was courteous enough to inquire about the family and her health, as usual, and asked why none of them ever wrote to me. My bewildered mother answered:

"You move too fast for us; we can't keep up with you and of course, you never write us, either. What is your new address?" It hadn't occurred to me that I was moving so frequently, as it seemed to me I was rather stationary lately. The lure of Nevada had me unwilling to move on to new territory quite yet.

Another venture came to mind — dealing cards and sharing (hopefully) in all that loose money in Nevada. With a lot of money, I reasoned, I could do a lot of things. It was worth a try, so I found the manager of one of the clubs and confessed to him that I didn't know how to deal cards but that I could sell poker chips. Ignorant of the fact that employees were not allowed to drink with any of the guests, or carry a half-pint in the chip-apron pocket, I soon learned that I had lost another job. The chips were certainly down!

Having a few tips in my pocket and my usual bottle, I set forth again for Los Angeles. I thought that if I were just half sober I could get a ride quicker. This was my lucky day, for a very nice, large, red-headed young man stopped his truck for me. As we rode along the busy highway, I emptied my bottle as we talked. He told me of his family, and I certainly told him about mine. He was such a sympathetic young man that he bought me a fifth of whiskey so as to ease the rest of the trip.

I was disgusted to learn on arrival at Pat's home that he had been arrested on a drunken charge again. I couldn't understand how he managed to secure whiskey while there was no food in the house for his children, but my sister-in-law explained that quickly. It seemed that Pat opened a charge account in my name at the liquor store a few blocks away, pledging my payment the next week-end. Imagine doing a thing like that! And just what week-end was he referring to? I wasn't living by a rigid schedule, for

I enjoyed and insisted on maintaining complete in-
dependence except when I needed some whiskey myself.   Having no sympathy left for Pat's weakness, I
decided not to waste any more time trying to help
him.   So, leaving him in jail I left town once more.

Never having seen the State Capitol at Sacramento,
I thought I would allow myself a special trip to see
the sights.   Taking a bus for this tour I planned a
stopover enroute, and immediately began searching
for a liquor store or bar for refreshment.   I then regretted having spent money on bus fare, for that same
money was needed at the bar.   I visited and drank in
all the bars in town for seven weeks, and invariably
on Saturday nights landed in jail.   However, I would
be free again each Sunday morning to resume another
week of squandering money my parents continued to
forward for my "Tour of the West".   I drank as much
during the weekdays as on Saturdays but Saturday
seemed to be my unlucky day.   This was also true for
the jailers as it seemed to them that I was inevitably
returning for regular visits.   During the week I found
myself a dingy room above bars or near them, and
occasionally the friendly bartender would send up a
drink for me.   This occurred when I was no longer
able to come down the flight of stairs, even for a drink.

Thus, I found my life surrounded and enveloped
with a force, like a mighty hurricane carrying high,
destructive winds, encircling and ripping my life to
shreds.   I was miserable with myself — feeling no hope
or desire to live any longer, as everything important to
me had vanished — maybe never to return.   Those old
feelings of being afraid to go to sleep and too miserable to stay awake prevailed again.   Fearful and tired
of people, disgusted with myself and particularly bored

with Saturday nights in that jail, I was ready to see the Capitol.

Accompanied by my usual lifeless companion, I resumed the trip to Sacramento, unaware of the dramatic, tragic incidents ahead for me and two future drinking acquaintances. Arrested on the first night in town, I awoke the next morning to hear a newsboy screaming the headline about a Southern girl being held as a material witness in the previous night's murder case. I managed to get a paper that someone had discarded (as I certainly hadn't a nickel left with which to buy one) to see if by some chance I knew the girl from my home state in such desperate need of help. I didn't think Southern girls were ever involved in such predicaments — not I, anyway. My arms were shaking so that I could hardly read the newspaper article, but I noticed her name to be the same as mine — I was shocked and puzzled, yet confident that I had been booked for drunkenness alone. It must be a mistake, I thought, as the girl written about in the paper had no address, just "transient" — address unknown. Still dazed and confused, delirium tremens starting, and following a flow of sweat and violent trembling, I fell unconscious.

When I awoke, whispers echoed through the cells as my inmates, people of all descriptions and booked on all charges, discussed the girl wanted in connection with the murder. In my vague mental condition I overlooked the fact that they were pointing at me, feeling sure it was a case of mistaken identity. Day after day I was called from my cell to be questioned about the murder, about which I knew absolutely nothing. For days, awaiting to be released, eager to be out and back on my scheduled drinking around the clock, I sat, uninformed of my part in the disastrous event.

With me in my cell were six other girls, two of whom were Mexicans, friendlier and kinder by far than the others. While I was in that miserable condition of trembling and vomiting, they took turns caring for me, and when the attack subsided they combed and fixed my hair. We chatted as they shared what cigarettes they had, exchanging descriptions of our girlhood. With all that time on our hands and little else to do but talk, I was interested in their native customs, and particularly how they made tortillas. Perhaps they were equally as interested in my traditions, but I couldn't share with them one important item: my name. I had completely forgotten it.

The Sacramento jail had unusually well-prepared food, and I knew I needed good nourishment, having neglected to eat properly for weeks and weeks, and finding little nourishment in most of the jails to which I had been committed. But the vibrating iron doors and the rattle and jingle of that bunch of keys sounded quite familiar. The routine of polishing and cleaning the bars, making our bunks and doing various other chores to comply with daily inspection was typical, and did little to soften the despair in which I found myself. If there's a hell on earth, I spent mine in those days and nights behind bars, sick and delirious, unable to recall my own name.

The oldest of the officers there was especially concerned for me, and he pulled me aside one afternoon and talked with me quite at length, as though I was his daughter. He warned me about the problem of alcohol, what it would do to me, in addition to the trouble I'd be in the rest of my life, if I didn't stop. After my most recent ordeal, I assured him that I'd never take another drink, and deep in my heart I meant to keep my promise.

The jailer finally appeared early one morning, telling me to get ready to appear in court. This was nothing new to me. I had quite often wired my father for money with which to pay a fine, and be on my careless way. But this court procedure seemed a bit different from the rest, and it truly embarrassed me that I didn't have positive identification or an address to give upon questioning — I had lost all memory of recent events. I had no recollection of having been in the mentioned bar the night a man had been dragged away and murdered. Many days and nights later, the criminals were captured and upon their confession, I was accompanied to the bus station and freedom, supplied with a lightweight coat and a ticket back to Stockton.

It was late in the afternoon when I boarded the bus for the short distance to Stockton, and as dark began to fall the impact of the past few days manifested itself as I crouched down in my seat, hiding behind the newspaper an officer had given me. Following his instructions to read about myself, I learned the details of the murder and my involvement, with a new fear. I was so afraid that I sat there tightly clenching the newspaper, holding it close to my face as if someone sitting nearby might see it and know that I was the girl involved. My mind was changing, wanting to forget the promise I had made to the fatherly police officer, for I relished the powerful and cunning effect of a drink.

I soon had ridden out my ticket and, choked with fear and remorse, I stood looking around inside the

Stockton station, expecting to be recognized by a policeman and taken away to that very familiar jail. Inasmuch as I had liked Stockton on my previous visit (despite the Saturday nights in jail) I was awed by my own fear of being there. I hadn't planned being away so long, and I was ready to catch up.

After wiring Mother for money again, I planned to get a room, get dead drunk and let life take its course. Uncertainty and anguish swelled up inside me, but in that gloomy little cabin which I leased upon receiving help from Mother, I was soon to find someone; the first to understand me, my problem, and its solution. In addition, I was to experience a great revelation.

The one-room cabin was situated between the owner's house and the railroad tracks, with a few yards of distance between, and its meager furnishings consisted of a narrow cot, a little night table, and a small clothes closet that provided a good pantry for my bottles, as I had on my only wardrobe. Through one of the tiny windows I could see my landlady's kitchen window a few yards away, and if I stood on my cot I could watch more closely to see if by any chance she was keeping an eye on me.

I had been secluded there several days, unseen by the landlady, when she came to inquire about me. I had left the cabin only for the short time required to scurry across the railroad tracks for a bottle of wine — like an animal in search of food. As the landlady, she had a right to be curious, although I had some misgivings about her visit. Perhaps she would ask me to leave, but regardless, I didn't welcome a visit from the landlady on any mission.

On answering her knock at the door I was surprised to see a truly beautiful woman, with rich, olive skin

and satin black hair. Her brown eyes were radiant as
I complimented her brilliantly-flowered dress, secretly
hoping to embarrass her into a hasty departure. As
she stood by the opened door, empty wine bottles from
the Mexican wine shop across the tracks where I had
frequently shopped, glared in the morning sunlight.
I really didn't want any intrusion, considered her
questions and conversation as prying, and openly resented her visit. She obviously pitied me as her eyes
moved from the empty bottles to my own. Then
she left. My rent was paid, so I hoped she wouldn't
interfere again and interrupt my drinking. Since I
was an outcast, I wanted to be left alone. Even the
cab driver was through with me, as I had pawned my
only pair of shoes to him for one more bottle of wine.

The day the landlady visited me I felt that Someone
somewhere was watching me, leaving me fearful and
accentuating my loneliness. I didn't think it was God,
as I had long ago decided that God wasn't in sympathy
with me; but when the landlady opened that door, a
ray of light came in that I didn't truly comprehend at
the time.

When wine, money and space for empty bottles ran
out, I reasoned that a crisis was at hand — something
had to change. At some time during my long journeys
and wanderings, I came to possess a little Testament,
and somehow it managed to keep up with me and my
excursions, but I hadn't opened it to read a word in
many a year.

I have never forgotten the long, miserable night in
that shabby little hut that had become my shell; the
night my wasted life began to catch up with me.
Reaching out convulsively for something to hold onto

during the darkest part of the night, my hand touched the little Bible on the table where I had laid it.

I casually picked it up and started reading the page to which it opened, and as I read along, something phenomenal filled my heart and soul. Being in the little room all alone, something spiritual or divine happened to cause the Book to fall open just there, and it was surely meant for me. Turning on the lamp, I began to read:

Save me, O God; for the waters are come in unto my soul.

I sink in deep mire, where there is no standing; I am come into deep waters, where the floods overflow me.

I am weary of my crying: my throat is dried: mine eyes fail while I wait for my God.

They that hate me without a cause are more than the hairs of mine head: they that would destroy me, being mine enemies wrongfully, are mighty: then I restored that which I took not away.

O God, thou knowest my foolishness; and my sins are not hid from thee.

Let not them that wait on thee, O Lord God of hosts, be ashamed for my sake: let not those that seek thee be confounded for my sake, O God of Israel.

Because for thy sake I have borne reproach; shame hath covered my face.

I am become a stranger unto my brethren, and an alien unto my mother's children.

For the zeal of thine house hath eaten me up; and the reproaches of them that reproached thee are fallen upon me.

When I wept, and chastened my soul with fasting,
    that was to my reproach.
I made sackcloth also my garment; and I became
    a proverb to them.
They that sit in the gate speak against me; and
    I was the song of the drunkards.

                Psalms 69:1-12

The passage was mortifying, and the solitude increased the awe I felt. I felt ashamed that my window sill lined with empty bottles could be so easily seen, a vivid reminder to God and man. In my near hysteria and remorse I called to my landlady, and she came immediately, running across the yard still tying her robe about her. After showing her what I had discovered in the Bible, she re-read it to me. When she had finished, she looked down at me as I sat on the edge of the bed, and reverently asked me if I believed in God, to which I answered, "Of course".

"Whether you do or not," she said, "He is surely watching over you." And in a calming voice she added, "Don't worry — everything is going to be all right now."

She continued to talk with me quietly and stayed with me until dawn and the sunshine came peeping through my window. As she sat looking at the sight of me, I knew she was wondering what she might do to help. Promising to return very shortly, she told me to relax while she fixed breakfast for her little adopted son, whom I had seen occasionally as he toddled about his little play yard.

Alone again, emotional upheaval raged in my mind and I wondered how I could make it to the wine

shop, get a bottle or just a single drink from the owner;
or if necessary, stagger on to bum one from somebody
else. I decided that my landlady was being too slow
returning to help me — and that perhaps she didn't
plan to return at all. In the torture, I just *had* to do
something for relief.

With what strength I could muster I forced myself
into the clothes I'd left lying across the end of the
cot, and half-way combing my mussed hair, I left the
room in a frenzy and actually began running across the
tracks to the wine shop. As I had been a regular
customer, the very accomodating proprietor gave me a
few drinks. My trembling relieved, I managed to return to my room. I could sit up straight again, and
I finished combing my hair as I slowly regained com-
posure.

The landlady returned within a few minutes, but
she stood silent for a few seconds as if wondering what
to say or how. I noticed that she had changed her
clothes, and being barefoot myself, her white mocca-
sins caught my eye momentarily as I suspected that her
attitude may have changed, too. I expected her to
ask me to move somewhere else, but instead, she put
her warm hand on mine and said:

"Honey, I have some friends who are members of a
club; a group of wonderful people who I believe can
help you. It is their purpose to help people in the
distress you suffer, and they are always happy to come
on call. Come on over to my house with me and let's
get you a hot bath and breakfast, now."

Well, I couldn't imagine anyone being interested
enough or wanting to help a stranger, but before I
could question her she was leading me out the door
toward her kitchen, adding that she had already called

the people and that they would be out that evening to visit with me.

Being dressed in a blue polka dot frock and wearing some slipper slides that she had given me, and having a fifth of wine that I intended to pay the Mexican for later, I was in fine shape when my visitors arrived that evening. They appeared to be quite nice people, a married couple and another lady, all of whom looked first at me and then at all those empty bottles. They introduced themselves as Mr. and Mrs. George Fairlane, and Miss Juanita Blair. Then the gentleman, with a hearty laugh worth a million dollars if you were in the mood to hear it (as I wasn't), asked, "How long have you been drinking?"

I didn't like his question or the implication in his voice, as I considered my actions my business and not theirs. I knew all along that they had come to pry into my personal affairs. I didn't want any interference, and certainly no preaching, but I felt it coming. As they kept looking and smiling, my temper boiled higher. I asked acidly, leaning against the door facing:

"What do you see from where you are that is so funny?"

Mr. Fairlane, from his casual stance, and with a tender smile now, said, "You remind us of what we used to be like, and the life we enjoy today. Certainly no offense was intended, as we would very much like to come inside and visit with you for a little while."

As they inched their way inside the minute room, I was hunting for words to inform them that I didn't care who they were or what they used to be like, for that matter. In my foul disposition, I didn't believe what they told me of their so-called "club" and its purposes and ideals, but I appreciated the fact that they were clean, happy, sober and respectable-looking.

I didn't like them, and as sick as I was I didn't want any more conversation. But they were eager to say more and wanted to say or do something to help me. One suggested that I was suffering from a real disease which she called "alcoholism".

"Well," I said, "I've never heard anything to top that. Can't you look at me and see for yourselves that I'm in perfect health? I've never even heard of that disease, and don't care to hear about it."

With such mysterious smiles on their faces, they must think I'm a real big joke, I thought. Regardless of what I said aloud or thought to myself, they stayed and stayed, talked and talked. I thought they would never leave so that I could finish that fifth of wine.

Finally, at the door to which I was urging them, they told me about a helpful and interesting book written by a man who once drank too much, and suggested that I read it. I emphasized my total disinterest in their club work and literary recommendations, and bade them farewell. But even as they walked away, they assured me that everything would be all right if I would accept their help. They also promised to be back the next day.

Quickly closing the door, almost in their faces, I lustily drained the half-empty wine bottle. I then changed back into my own clothes, and deciding to give the borrowed shoes a little exercise, I treated myself to another trip across the tracks to the wine shop. I confided in the little Mexican, told him of my pending move to a nearby town, and pledged that I would pay my bill as soon as money came from my mother.

So, I slipped out of the cabin after dusk and wired for some money with which to buy some clothes, telling not an entire untruth about losing everything I had. If I didn't get some shoes soon, I really would have pneumonia, I thought. I did manage to buy some sandals so as to conform with the majority of people in California, and headed for the highways again, continuing my endless search for somebody, somewhere, with genuine understanding; completely ignoring the efforts of assistance from my most recent acquaintances from that club with the funny-sounding name, a mouthful to think and harder to say, Alcoholics Anonymous.

IV

HITCHING A SOFT-TOUCH

I kept in touch with my family in Los Angeles periodically and managed to see them every six months or so, conforming with my lax schedule. I hitched a ride back on a truck (I was beginning to admire the Californian truck drivers for their generosity). When I arrived for my overdue visit with them, I was a dirty mess, full of black smoke and splattered with tar from the hot, nearly liquid asphalt highways, all ready and able to give them my devoted assistance. I couldn't be of much help, as usual, and I was too late besides — as I found them getting ready to move, upon the request of their landlord. They were three months behind with the rent, swamped with overdue household bills and of course, owed a large sum to the liquor store, too. I was disgusted more than ever with Pat, and very disappointed that he hadn't provided for his family better than he had — or at all.

To add further humiliation to the scene, he "passed out" on the couch, only half-clad in a ragged undershirt, soiled khaki trousers and one house shoe, unable to help with the moving. Thinking myself invulnerable, I wanted to help this family, and as long as I had a bottle for personal support I was able to help meet some of the expenses with more "temporary" jobs. Thinking of this man, my own half brother, neglecting his responsibility to such a fine family, added to my already mountainous disapproval of men, in general.

I occasionally gave a little thought to the possibility of a husband at some time in the future. Now, mainly to help my family of nieces, I hoped to find a man with plenty of money and sympathy. That's what we needed, all right. The right man would be the answer to all our prayers and needs. Now, could I find this man to solve all our complex problems, and yet who possessed the desirable qualifications of a man I could really admire and respect? Pondering these questions, I stood on the edge of the highway, enveloped in smog and waiting for a ride; a ride to greener pastures again.

The day wasn't one of my lucky ones, obviously, and I grew bitter toward all the drivers passing me by. Didn't they know I wanted a ride to look for a job for my expressed purpose of helping my destitute family? I muttered under my breath that all these people were selfish and really mean not to pick me up and thereby improve the circumstances just that much. However, the gin and lime were in me, softly clouding the several hours of waiting in the hot sun.

A candy salesman came along eventually and at his invitation, I sampled the candy wares as we sped along. When we parted some hours later my stomach was churning violently — booze and all that chocolate confection didn't seem to mix very well. My riding with him in that little old two-door Chevy had let one Californian do his good deed for the day, I thought. Feeling some satisfaction I transferred my miserable self to another spot on the highway to wait for another ride.

I waited for many hours; hours that seemed to drag more slowly in my wretched condition, made worse by my being in such a hurry to do something for the family. I had told Pauline that I would return that evening with some money from somewhere, perhaps from a friend. What friend? What friend with money? I didn't know where I thought I'd get the money, but I was in a hurry to get out and look for it. While waiting for some generous soul to pick me up, I remembered my vow to help her care for the girls.

At long last the second ride for the seemingly endless day came along. The driver, an apparently nice man, asked me where I was going in such a condition. He asked if I wasn't afraid to wait so near the highway in such heavy fog and wasn't I afraid, taking such a chance as a woman alone? I thought him rather inquisitive. Then I decided I could answer all his questions and gain his sympathy at the same time with one simple answer:

"My half brother in Los Angeles and I had a squabble, and after that I couldn't stay in the same house with him a day longer — he's just a selfish alcoholic."

(How could we have had a squabble — we were never out of jail and home at the same time!)

The driver asked me to talk plainer as he hardly understood my drawl, so I tried a little harder to impress him. He insisted on discussing me. He asked why I was drinking and why so much. At this, I decided he was definitely prying into my personal business too much, and told him so in very plain language. When my last drink was gone, I threatened to get out of his car if he didn't buy me another bottle at the very next store. With such a threat, how could he lose? Nonetheless, he did stop and he swore that it was the first time he had ever been inside a liquor store.

Well, I had assumed he was a foreigner when I

learned his name was Val Martinelli, and his amazing innocence substantiated my guess. But, I surmised, his flashy green and white coupe represented many a dollar not dedicated to whiskey purchases. In addition to my other observations, I noted that he was a handsome, well-dressed man, with coal-black hair and dark, keen eyes — inquisitive — but nice.

After a few drinks from the new bottle, I began to think this man a pretty swell fellow — so generous, concerned and considerate. I volunteered to continue riding with him as far as he was going. For the next three hours he told me about himself; of his commercial boat docked at the next city where he was to meet a crowd of his fellow employees from the city hall. They were going on a deep sea fishing trip on his craft. He asked me if I'd like to go along, and after proving to me that he wasn't married by permitting me to call his office, I accepted his invitation to accompany him and his friends, many of whom were married couples. We explained my impromptu presence by saying that I was a friend of his sister's, visiting her from the South. I surely couldn't hide my Southern drawl, but with my sluggish enunciation I helped partly to fib our way out of a surprising and dubious situation; for Val's friends had long ago given him up as a hopeless bachelor.

Everyone seemed to have had a wonderful day at sea, and we returned to the dock late in the evening, loaded with three hundred pounds of assorted fish, several empty liquor bottles (compliments of the guests) and a mighty sick gal on board.

Several days later I divulged the entire truth of my disappearance to Pauline — about the day that began as "unlucky", no rides, and no money; but ended happily with a very nice gentleman who entertained his guests and cared for their fish, while I cared for the whiskey bottles — all on a deep sea fishing trip.

Six months later, upon inquiry about the state of affairs of Pat's family, I learned that though he was back in jail, the rent had been paid, groceries and supplies were in sufficient quantity, and the accumulated household bills had been liquidated. It was a comfortable life for Pat's family and me while my future husband helped care for them.

Over the period of the next nine or ten months, Pat and I had it made for sure. Val was waiting for me to get sober and stay sober before our marriage. During this time he was willing for me to stay at Pat's and every other night he drove some forty miles to see how I was progressing with my now spasmodic drinking. As Val was paying the rent, grocery and liquor bills, we didn't want for anything, and hardly missed Pat when he was absent from the comfortable household — back in jail. When Christmas rolled around that year those little girls had the biggest Santa Claus they had ever known, thanks to Val.

I never fully met Val's requirements, but finally we were married by a minister at a quiet ceremony in Las Vegas. The wedding was attended by two witnesses whom we invited after making their casual acquaintance in a restaurant. They seemed delighted to grant the favor. I had chosen to wear a beautiful pale blue woolen suit with dark blue accessories, and Val presented me with a lovely corsage of Sweetheart roses. Upon convincing him that I had to have a half-pint to ease my wedding-day tensions, I swore that if he'd buy it for me, I'd never ask for another as long as I lived.

I nursed that half-pint until we reached Pat's house again after the nuptials. I couldn't wait to get to that liquor store around the corner to load up, but Pat had beaten me to the draw. Expecting us to return for a celebration after our marriage, he had two uncorked fifths of bourbon waiting when we arrived.

Pat had many good reasons for asking us to stay a day or two, and I agreed that the ten-month courtship and ultimate marriage certainly warranted more than one mere cocktail in its culmination. But my new husband, with much vexation, must have been greatly relieved when the liquor and our welcome had expired. So with great flourish on his part, we departed for our new home.

Val and I rented an efficiency apartment in a very elaborate motel, with luxurious furnishings and fine services. In the only home I had known in so long, I was typically ecstatic as I attended to my wifely duties, preparing special dishes as I cooked, keeping the apartment spic and span — all in the way I felt a good wife should. I enjoyed my new role, as long as it lasted, but I soon added drinking to my little heaven. Then I discovered the Santa Anita race track which, combined with my regular tour of elegant bars, made for a busy day. I hurried on my rounds in order to be back at the suite when Val returned from work, and despite the inconvenient rush to return to my domestic duties, I had it made.

During the next year of my marriage, neither Pat nor I knew a sober moment. I was going through Val's life savings and weekly earnings like a tornado — at the race track, in liquor stores and bars, and via various charge accounts. As Mrs. Martinelli, the wife of a good fellow who would stand behind his wife's bills, I didn't want for a thing. So many new clothes alone would have made any other woman grateful. Neither did my friends and relatives want for anything when I knew of their needs.

While at the race track, I became well acquainted with a couple, and in my drunken condition I boasted to them about my patient, considerate and generous husband. I wanted them to come home with me to meet him soon. They were in circumstances similar to mine prior to my marriage to Val — just enough clothes for decency but plenty of yen for liquor. They rented a tiny little shack, one room furnished with a double bed, a little table and two chairs sitting on the bare cement floor. An electric percolator sat on the table, and in one corner of the tiny room was a crock of olives which they had picked and put up for fermenting. After several visits at their room, we finally introduced ourselves, and on learning that they were Mr. and Mrs. Louis Warren, I was sure they were related to some of the Warrens I had known back in the South. We had a lot in common, it seemed, so we talked and talked for five days as I kept them and myself well supplied with all the liquor I could carry. I was enjoying good credit at a liquor store situated conveniently between my suite and their shack, and as soon as Val left for work, I left too; keeping the same hours that he did.

Val began wondering after several weeks of marriage where I was spending these days, getting so drunk that I was unable to fix his supper. He knew that the half-pint to which he supposedly limited me per day couldn't make me "pass out", so he discovered that we three were drinking and clinging together like leeches. I calculated that he would be unaware of the amount of whiskey purchases until he received the bill, by which time his objections would be "too late", and even expected that he would stop my credit at the store on learning the extent of my misguided generosity.

When he did receive the bill, he tossed it on the bed and said:

"I'm about ready to give up. I never bought liquor before you entered my life, let alone on credit. You'll have to pay this yourself. I'm ashamed to face 'Happy'. We've known each other all our lives, and you're embarrassing me. I didn't mind paying your bills for awhile to keep my credit rating good. However, I refuse to continue facing him, paying your bills."

The nickname "Happy" truly suited the little Italian; a very small, black-haired, black-eyed, chattery man with a heavy accent that really fascinated me. I spent many carefree hours laughing and gabbing with "Happy" over the counter, sharing outlandish tales. He surely must have appreciated the steady patronage from this lush, the wife of one of his oldest friends.

Val thought it would hurt my pride and make me ashamed to pay "Happy's" bill myself with his check, but he was pitifully disillusioned. My credit standing remained ace high. I was delighted to be able to pay such an enormous liquor bill, after having skipped out on many a smaller one. Val worked every day of the week to meet my liquor needs and other credit obligations which I incurred with complete confidence in what I believed to be his unlimited resources and unlimited devotion.

A carnival was due to open in a nearby town, to which I invited my drinking companions to attend as guests of my husband and myself. Val was somewhat older than I and not interested in going to the "mid-way", but I threatened to leave him if he didn't be a good sport and host by taking my Southern friends and me over to the carnival. He arranged to take half a day off work and escorted three drunks. Following introductions he asked if all Southerners were drunk-ards — all he'd met thus far surely were. On finding himself in the company of my friends who had taken advantage of him through me, he became more ex-asperated and reluctant.

I'm sure the day at the carnival will remain as vivid in his memory as in mine, as it was as much torture for him as it was riotous fun for the rest of us. I acted like a child while covering the grounds, going from the giant ferris wheels to the wild, twisting vehicles; munching candy apples and picking at the cotton candy.

Reminding Val of my serious threat, I ushered us all toward The Glass House. Once inside, with dress tails flying, doors slamming, floors shaking and a mil-lion deceiving mirrors, he couldn't catch my hand to steady himself or outwit any of the contraptions de-vised for this "crazy house". I thought it all so funny as the planned course became rougher all along; but Val's temper rose higher and higher, reminding me of a bull in a china shop. We reached the top of the inclined route at last, and he immediately dropped in exhaustion on a little chair planted beneath a sign purposely inviting one to "have a seat". After a scant second, the rigged chair turned him every way; up, down, around and around, and finally loose onto a long sliding board, and down he slid, tumbling over and over ridiculously to the bottom. The three drunks followed with great delight down the slide, much to his chagrin.

Val was furious yet sullen as we drove toward home; enroute I saw a sign advertising a palmist salon on the road ahead. I had always wanted to have my fortune told, but it required additional threats to persuade him to stop at the reader's.

The gypsy read my palm and told me some things I didn't know or even slightly believe. I was sober enough to recognize her obviously ambiguous statements, but she predicted some things I already knew or vaguely suspected. Looking at the life lines on my trembling hand, she said:

"Your marriage isn't going to last much longer. I see much unhappiness in your future, and travel to faraway places."

These were not surprising revelations to me because I needed no crystal ball for the information in the first place. I knew it wouldn't be long until Val would be filled with disgust and find life with me repulsive. I no longer felt absolutely assured of his devotion, and realized that I had failed, possibly never to gain his respect. The carnival incident added another straw to break his strong endurance.

The bar near the race track was my most favored, for I admired its many fabulous furnishings. The exquisite crystal chandeliers and the magnificent walnut bar imbedded in plush velvet carpet created an atmosphere which seemed to command proper behavior from the patrons. No monkey stuff was allowed — you acted civil, or out you went. Conversations including horse race discussions, were carried on in hushed tones, from famous personages (some of whom I recognized) on down to bookies and ordinary customers like me. I made the acquaintance of all sorts of people during my frequent patronage, some of whom I found to be quite interesting; and with some I found much in common. The Warrens "from the South" were among my first companions, but due to my "frequency", my circle enlarged rapidly.

I realized I had seen a particular girl many times previous to our actual introduction as we sat side by side at the bar. I couldn't believe all she proceeded to tell me — her descriptions and even her basic conversation was so far-fetched that I decided she was either full of bull or full of booze. Such distrust and lack of comprehension is typical of alcoholism, but even so, she found in me a willing though dubious listener to her every word.

The girl said she was the wife of a famous jockey; famous even to my uninformed ears. I was quick to recognize that she possessed many expensive jewelry ensembles, always complementing her classic taste in clothes that became her small frame. I couldn't imagine that a popular jockey's wife would socialize with a nonentity in a public bar, but alcoholism is no respecter of person — big or little, rich or poor. We frequently met at the bar for the following several days, becoming well acquainted as we sat drinking and impressing one another. I told her that my husband held an enviable post with the city, and likewise exaggerated the salary in proportion to the ficticious position. But before many drinks, I pleaded a temporary state of financial embarrassment and suggested she buy me a few drinks to tide me over 'til our next meeting when I would surely reciprocate. I discounted everything she told me about herself, her husband's tremendous salary, and the increasing demand for his services as a jockey, though I conceded that he was famous and capable. I usually didn't believe anything or anybody, not even myself on many occasions; so why should I believe another drunk barfly?

Shortly thereafter, I went to the bar to meet her as usual and was surprised to find that she was not waiting at our favorite table. I inquired if she had been in on her daily visit, but received no answer. Then I noticed that the bar and even the adjoining restaurant were unusually quiet for that hour. The talkative bartenders were suddenly silent, unwilling to say a word in answer to my questions, though they had previously narrated extensively that the owner of the illustrious establishment was the jockey of whom I had been hearing so much (and whose name shone in bright neon lights overhead); and that the girl with whom I had become friends was the jockey's wife. I had written them off as more imaginative drunks, too. (Bartenders there were usually drunk, anyway.)

I moved to another part of the lounge in search of my girlfriend, and on passing where the bookies had gathered, I was shocked to learn that the jockey had been thrown from his horse and fatally injured. Trying to sort the facts from the fiction was getting to be a complicated problem, but I resolved to figure it out for myself, deeming that the factors to disprove my girl-friend's status in the case were available somewhere.

The tragedy was the talk of the entire town and on hearing that a western movie star was to sing at the funeral, I saw the opportunity to kill two birds with one stone — prove the girl a liar and at the same time see the popular singer. So, picking up my Southern friends, the Warrens, we three stood at a respectful distance from the ceremony, yet close enough to see.

For the occasion, Louis Warren decided to keep on his riding breeches and boots so that in the event the cowboy did sing at the jockey's funeral, he would be appropriately attired. Lucy Warren seemed to have no choice but to wear her seersucker slacks, so, just like old times, I followed suit to the extent that I was sporting some new ones.

To my amazement and ultimate sorrow, the girl was there at the graveside in proper mourning attire, and I was finally convinced that she had been telling me the truth after all. I managed to catch a glimpse of the western idol as he rode his beautiful white horse away, but by my own undoing, I don't remember hearing him sing "There's a Gold Mine in the Sky".

The actual truth had to be proven, regardless of the issue. The world was full of phonies I couldn't trust — just like myself.

Attempting to issue an ultimatum, Val accused me of causing him nearly to lose his job after twenty-three years of continuous service. No doubt my ill-timed notion to call his boss and cry on his shoulder about Val's habitual drinking, because of which our marriage was floundering, caused quite a shock at city hall. I couldn't explain to Val what had possessed me to strike such a low blow to his good standing, but it was evidently the result of my own inner conflict as well as for seeking revenge. I had grown increasingly and selfishly wary of Val's pleas to stop drinking and stay home.

"You leave me no alternative," he said, with obvious suffering, "but it's you who's forcing me to make this decision. I'm going to send you off on a vacation to sober up and reform permanently — or else I'll have to divorce you, and you know that is contrary to my religious beliefs. I'm giving you one more chance to save our marriage — if you call it that."

Val suggested a lovely place in the country with new surroundings and people conducive to my recovery, little knowing how much territory I had already covered and the time I had wasted on similar missions of good intent. But with all my heart I wanted to make amends and atone for the unhappiness I had inflicted upon my generous and exploited husband. When I consented to make another try, he hesitated to tell me that he had planned for his spinster sister to chaperone me during the allotted six months' vacation. Reservations had been made in advance for a most comfortable, two bedroom, spacious and quite adequately furnished cabin nestled among pines bending with the breeze from the lake. Even though I resented the burden of having Maria shadow me, Val's description of the remote, unpublicized and therefore unspoiled resort, was appealing. We were prepared and eager to start out early the next morning.

I found I liked Val's sister very much, and in particular her Italian habit of including wine in all three daily menus. I remembered that many a day wine alone was the menu, not just the appetizer or complement. Thus the rehabilitation program was off to a bad start from the first meal we shared together. Maria had treated me to her specialty, and the lasagna should have highlighted the supper, but I was all too ready and eager to display my amazing prowess in alcohol consumption.

The cabin site overlooked the beautiful, placid lake, creating an air of utmost serenity. I was anything but placid as I alternately paced the cottage, the grounds and the lake front in utter boredom and torment. I had packed a couple of pints of whiskey in my suit-cases for the dire emergencies I was sure to face when I could no longer tolerate my agonizing thirst — I was yielding fast. Adding the tempting wine to my rations, I stayed close to our comfortable quarters for the first two days. Finally I surrendered completely to the supreme, powerful enemy in my life and the lives around me.

As we had driven through town the day of our arrival, I spotted the nearest source of liquor. While there two days later placing my order for a fifth of gin and tossing down a few cocktails to quench my immediate thirst, I shared with the other patrons and barflies the saddest news of the day — the death of President Franklin Roosevelt. His death had occurred in Warm Springs, Georgia, and even though the town was close to my own home town, I felt sure that my folks hadn't heard the news. Maria and I had heard the first newscast bulletin together over the radio in the cabin, but on the pretense of hunting a telephone to call home, I had gotten away from her at last and out on the town. Using familiar old tactics, I explained to my new bar friends that I was a stranger to their lovely locale and somewhat lonely and bored, having come to the lake with my relative, who was recuperating from major surgery. There was no need for any of the prevarications, but that sort of imagination had become a habit; for Maria enjoyed superb health, evidenced by her statuesque frame, vibrant personality and sparkling blue eyes. Before many hours of vacation had passed she became quite exasperated with her charge and mission.

Upon my return to the cabin after making that phone call, dawn was just a few hours away. Maria met me in the small living room, stopped abruptly in front of me and emphasized indignation by putting her hands on her hips.

"Well, you've been gone long enough to go all the way to Georgia and save yourself the long distance call. Your lies haven't fooled me — it's quite obvious that you're drunk again, and not even trying to resist it. Val loves you so much despite this weakness. I don't see how you can be so selfish and unconcerned. You could at least try after all he's done for you, including this vacation treat," she argued, "to make his life and yours worth living. You're wrecking his life as well as yours, and I just can't stand by and watch you do it. I'm ready to go home."

In my sad condition, I admitted to Maria and myself that even if the folks had been present at the President's bedside, they would never think to let me know of the whole nation's loss; I wasn't worth the effort. I tried to apologize to her, and pleaded with her to stay at the lake with me, but Maria had little patience and sympathy for me. She insisted on phoning Val to come for us immediately, sparing time and cost of explanations via her own long distance call, for he would know exactly what had happened and hasten to her rescue. So I knew that I, too, must hurry in order to make another trip to the liquor store and return before Val's arrival.

As we left the resort in the re-packed automobile, I noticed the sad expressions of those two faces in the front, and I tried to console them as I slumped on the rear seat. I overlooked my own contribution to their double disappointment, and assured them that our nation would soon have another President.

We were all silent for the remainder of the trip

until we deposited Maria at her home. Alighting from the car and waiting beside it until Val transferred her luggage to the porch, she leaned down to the car window and said to me:

"I'm truly sorry that the vacation hasn't had the desired results for you and Val, but I do hope you can get over this ridiculous behavior of yours for his sake. And I'm sorry that we couldn't have had a pleasant vacation together, for you know I needed it; my life hasn't been as idle as yours."

Then she marched up the walk, flanked on either side by a galaxy of white petunias, to her beautiful house. Though smaller in size, it closely resembled an ante-bellum home surrounded by tall, white columns. She resumed her justified "silent treatment" for over a month, at the end of which she broke that tension and invited us to come to her home for a spaghetti supper.

As Maria was a very refined and gracious person, possessing quiet charm becoming her middle age, I yearned to please her. By toasting to a new vow that I could prove myself to be a real lady the night of the dinner invitation and reconcile myself to Val and his sister, I over-indulged to the extent that I could hardly stand up on arrival; or much less manage the spaghetti onto my fork. I did quite well with the traditional wine Maria felt compelled to serve as an earlier course, which made an ungracious and therefore most unwelcomed guest of me, in spite of my good intentions.

As Val led me toward the foyer, Maria meant her admonition as she said to him, "This will be your last invitation to my home until you can come alone. I'm very sorry, Val, but I just can't take your wife's behavior. You're my brother and I love you very much, but I feel you have been victimized by this young, immature woman. I hope you will forgive me for my own intolerance."

Getting up earlier than usual the morning following the preceding incident, I noticed a peculiar expression on Val's face as he was putting on his clothes to leave for work. That expression would have caused anyone to take heed. Looking at me from his tired, circled eyes and with a bit of anger in his tone, he said:

"Do you know that you've been rambling through this apartment all night long, and I haven't slept a wink?"

I didn't say, but his sleeping or lack of it was not my primary concern; but the lost bottle of whiskey was. I had hidden it from myself and had completely forgotten where, so I had searched for it all night long. But attempting to be sympathetic, I took his hand and apologized for keeping him awake all night. I also attempted to con him into getting me one more half-pint so that I could get my clothes on, comb my hair and help him off to work. This would begin another day of torment. I didn't get too far with him that early in the morning as he, too, was now giving me the silent treatment. Holding his hand, I told him I couldn't get dressed until he got it for me, but pushing me away, he said:

"If I got it for you, you'd never get your clothes on, much less fix my breakfast."

I promised never to take another drink or do anything again to hurt him. Besides, if he'd get it now he wouldn't have to bring my half-pint at lunch, which had been my daily allotment since our marriage. I didn't realize that Val couldn't get my whiskey until the liquor store opened, for my mind was concentrated on another puzzle — where had I put that bottle.

Resting his arm on my shoulder and looking into my half-open eyes, he said, "Honey, do you realize what you're doing to me, and our marriage? Can't you realize that you're killing yourself and breaking up our home at the same time? I'm completely at my road's end — I don't know what to do with you."

I wondered what he intended to do as he was already late for work. Time was passing mighty slowly for me as I stood still eyeing the clock, thinking that he'd better hurry and make up his mind.

After another hour of his silence while pacing the floor, with me pacing right behind him, he nonchalantly opened our front door and left the room. I couldn't take the reticence much longer in my deprived condition, so I cared not that perhaps he was leaving for good. He sauntered down our long walk, strolling back and forth and once in a while looking at his watch.

Finally stopping under the living room window, he started watering my roses that he had planted for me when we first rented our apartment. He wasn't aware that I was watching from the big picture window, giving him just thirty more minutes to make up his mind whether or not he was going to get that liquor.

Time was marching on for us both, yet he was still checking his watch and I was worrying simultaneously about his being late for work and the bar opening for business within a few minutes. All the beautiful things that he had given me were for the birds, I thought at the time. I had to consume more and more alcohol — it had become the supreme rule of my life, and must somehow be obeyed to the fullest extent. I didn't like any sort of reprimand, but he knew I especially disliked being ignored. It was a question of who was tormenting whom.

Calling him to the window in the pitiful tone I thought might penetrate him, I pleaded for him to get it for me this one more time, again promising to quit drinking and try to make a go of our marriage and make him happy. One more half-pint wouldn't hurt me, and shouldn't hurt him to go get it. He shut off the water faucet and decided to come inside, bringing in a fragrant, long stemmed rosebud for the coffee table. He approached me, puffing his cigar as usual, and deposited me beside him on the floral print covered sofa. Trying to hold my trembling hand even as I halfheartedly rejected him, he said:

"I'm getting older now and I would like to have a little peace of mind in my old age but it certainly looks hopeless for me — you're too wrapped up in your selfishness to want to share your life with me, and you should realize that my terms are not unreasonable."

I actually heard very little he said as my mind was still in a whirl, still trying to remember where on earth I'd stashed that bottle the night before. Hiding a bottle from myself was something I had never done before, and I couldn't begin the search for my hidden treasure until he left for work. He was already over an hour late and I was really in a quandary.

I wondered if he was planning another secluded vacation for me or perhaps planning to just walk out on me. Had I been able to have a "few" I could have figured it all out, and could certainly have gotten him to the job on time. Val was staring intensely at me, and the arduous tug at my arm interrupted my inebriated imagination when he sweetly said:

"Baby, you could be every bit as sweet as that rose lying on the table if you'd try a little harder. Why won't you really stop drinking right now — for me — not later." I remained totally unresponsive. Whirling around on his heels as he rose, he announced, "I'll be back later."

My temper boiled higher when he neglected to tell me if he was going to that liquor store or to work, or where. At last he departed in the car, giving me time to resume my scavenging, but I didn't disturb too many things in looking for my bottle. I figured he just might sneak back earlier than noontime, and my calculations were right.

Two hours later he returned home, choosing to park at the curb and walk up the driveway, picking and tossing leaves disgustedly in the air as he approached the apartment. I thought surely one of us had gone goofy, as he'd never behaved this way before. It was he and not I, for he handed me a half-pint of whiskey at the door.

Without a word, he took the cap off the bottle and handed it to me. I couldn't imagine what was coming next, after his complete "about face", but with a big drink I could at least try to unscramble this strange turn of events. Holding my other hand, he almost proudly said,

"Honey, now you see? You've waited this long for this bottle and I know now that you are doing better, and just this much makes me hopeful in a future for us both."

Poor, innocent soul, little did he know how baffling that half-pint was as he left for work with a big smile on his face. That one big drink was so mysteriously powerful that I could now braid my hair, get dressed and walk straight to that bottle I had hidden the night before. It was neatly tucked in Val's overcoat pocket, placed in a cedar bag for the winter — it should have been forever. Cunning, baffling and powerful enough to completely control my mental and physical capacities.

I was pulling some uncanny tricks on Val these days, although he was happy in the belief that I had gone long hours without a drink and felt sure that my road to recovery was paved. Little did he know how long it was, as I slyly continued my drinking, noting his pleasure as I greeted him when he walked in for lunch the following and a few subsequent days. The pleasure was mutual because under his arm he always tucked a newspaper to disguise my half-pint bottle from the neighbor's view. They were especially nosey lately, openly and verbally wondering why Val had been staying home so much for the past few days. He may have been embarrassed, but he was also delighted to find me alert, for a change, and capable of preparing tasty lunches to share in the dinette. He praised the spaghetti I often fixed according to his expert directions.

Val was unaware that "Happy" was still one of my best friends and that my trips to his store had grown more frequent, bringing in all the bottles that I could safely hide from his ramblings to find them. The full pint size was not as easily concealed as half-pints as I could squeeze them between the cotton batting and plastic covers of cushions on our porch. We didn't sit on the porch much anyway, so I just ripped the seams in the cushions, slid my bottles in between, and sewed

the seam back again. I had it made for at least one
season — cunning, baffling and powerful.

Val had a week or two of contentment while I was
at least sober enough to stay on my feet. I was carefree and very content with having a full supply stored
away, plus my additional half-pint at lunch every day.
For a short while I didn't even need to see "Happy".
Val was walking on air. I added more feathers to my
cap, and still more when he called my family to tell
them the good news of the progress I was making.
Via our telephone they shared the happiness together
with a long telephone conversation; not a "collect"
one. I thought a big celebration was in order after
the good news was relayed to my family — but not
that night. It was more important that I stay on my
feet to get Val off to work on time the next morning,
and above all, that I go see "Happy". I would take
him the good news about my success and bring back
enough half-pints which, if pre-treated just right, could
be placed in the upper compartment of the commode.
I wouldn't dare put over two as more might interfere
with flushing the commode. Once before, the bottles
had floated on top and caused a big plumbing bill,
due to the labels coming off and clogging up the flush
mechanism — this I didn't want to happen again. I
was working so hard and regular each day, devoting
much time to finding and developing additional hiding
places. I was at ease for several days, managing to
get along with the lunchtime delivery and managing
to be a good wife, too. Deep inside I felt contented
and comfortable with the assurance of a supply on
hand in case of another crisis. However, the crisis was
near.

A week or so later when my hidden supply had

diminished, Val found me sleeping at noon and I couldn't be budged with a cannon — no lunch prepared — no nothing. I had passed out across the bed.

I inadvertently missed Val's lunch visit one day when a community doctor visited me instead. He had entered, uninvited, by the side patio door and stood just inside, calling me. Shocked by the presence of someone in the house, I answered with the usual series of questions I suppose: Who are you? Why are you here? Why didn't you knock first?

"Young lady," he said, looking over his horn rimmed glasses and proceeding down the hall, "Val told me you were hard to awaken and when you didn't answer my knocking, I thought I'd enter, as he wanted me to see you immediately. He seemed pretty worried about you."

The doctor surely did see me immediately, meeting me halfway down the hall, at which point I had haphazardly slipped into my housecoat and slippers, but as usual, my uncombed hair was in a million tangles.

"I'm Dr. Murray", he said in a very apologetic voice, "and I'm sorry to startle you, but aren't you sleeping rather late, anyway?" He set his little black satchel on the small night table within my reach. I sat down on the edge of the bed as ordered, at the same time asking what he wanted to see me about. I didn't need a doctor, but on second thought, perhaps I needed what a doctor could give me to relieve my new seige. My eyes and thoughts were glued to that black bag. He said he had come to see about me, and if he was sent to help me, I wanted his help first and we'd talk health and medicine later — and looking straight into his eyes, I told him so.

He asked how long my nerves had been in such a

shape, and unaware that I sounded unnerved, I answered abruptly, "all my life". Unzipping the black bag and holding a little juice glass full of water to my mouth, he ordered, "Now swallow this little pill with the water — it'll settle your nerves within a few minutes, because I have to get some important facts over to you, and you must be able to listen."

I would have swallowed anything to relieve my torment that day of misery. He held my hand gently in his until that sedative took effect, and speaking kindly, he said, "Let me do the talking and you do the listening."

He must have been psychic, for it was usually the other way around.

"Val is one of my closest and oldest friends and I must advise you that if you don't give up whiskey, you'll have to give him up. I could help you shake the whiskey if you'd help yourself — and keep Val. He's a pretty good guy, you know."

My temper boiled as I told Dr. Murray about some of my drinking, but that Val had exaggerated and divulged personal business to a strange doctor. With this flare up, Dr. Murray handed me two more Red Birds (sedatives) and promised that I'd feel better in another few minutes; then he found me quite talkative. While I talked he was writing me a prescription for thirty-six Red Birds, diagnosing my case as a "very nervous inward condition".

Calling Val from the dinette telephone he explained his theory and advised Val to take a few days off work in order to personally administer his prescription together with a series of mineral baths, confident that I'd soon be well again. I was willing to follow Dr. Murray's instructions only because he was one of Val's best friends, not because I expected or desired a cure. As I walked with him toward the living room door, he told me Val planned an early start on the mineral baths, and thanks to the doctor's short visit I had ample time for a five-hour nap.

Val, so innocent, so willing, hurried home that evening, stopping first at a nearby drugstore to get my prescription filled before our departure that night. In case I became sick on the way, the new medicine would surely help until we arrived in Mineral Springs, some ninety miles away. I didn't see much enroute (I slept all the way, unnaturally) and was thoroughly relaxed when we arrived at the springs. Then, after I had changed into my pajamas, Val graciously attended by handing me the bottle from which to take my two "Red Birds". Dr. Murray's prescription soon caused me to pass out for another very good night's sleep.

The combination of two sulphur baths a day and the prescription made it increasingly more difficult for me to get down two flights of cement steps into the large individual pool. The pool was made so as to enable the bather to adjust the temperature of the water by simple hydrants. However, either hot, cold, or any variation suited me in my numbed condition, as the bottle of "Red Birds" never left my possession.

Val thought that I was sure to improve from so much sleep, rest, and mineral baths, plus medicine that Dr. Murray prescribed, but I had bargained only to do as Dr. Murray had asked then — not forever. The last few weeks of our marriage were miserable. I was either asleep all day and up all night; or up all day drinking, and passed out at night. Val had done all he could do alone. Dr. Murray's visit was his last line of defense, but Val, not having experience with drunks until I crossed his path, found the fifteen months we were married a hopeless waste of life and love.

During my travels, drinking along the way, I had associated with all kinds of drunkards. Considering this fact, a specimen like Louis Warren should not have been unusual, but he was the most repulsive, vulgar, and dirtiest drunk that I had ever seen. During our acquaintance of approximately two months, I don't believed he ever bathed or changed his clothes. He especially sickened his wife, Lucy, and occasionally she would succeed in getting him at least to shave, but after a week he was his bear-like self again.

I liked pert little Lucy very much, though I didn't understand why she had married such a disgusting beast. It seemed to me that the only common bond they shared was alcohol, and in pity for Lucy, I figured she must need a lot of it to stomach him.

When Lucy and I had settled ourselves on bar stools one day in our favorite bar, Louis straddled another much further down the line. To this act we certainly did not protest. Lucy, knowing his disposition, asked me to help her keep an eye on him.

Louis leaned across the counter and looked squarely into the eyes of the sturdy looking but impassive bartender, and drew his fist back in a kidding, drunken way, and said, "Give me a big drink — and while you're at it, 'Big Boy,' give me a big smile to match it!"

The busy bartender handed him a drink, but with a vicious expression he said, "Big Stuff, drink that drink in a hurry — and then let me miss you, or I'll throw you straight out that door. I've told you ten times to spare us your presence, and now I mean it. Drink this one and get out."

Lucy and I had been too busy visiting around in the lounge at other times to have noticed or heard the threats, but we were at the final scene when Louis had become more furious and obnoxious, and bullying that giant bartender, he said, "I've already warned you. Her husband", pointing at me, "is a close friend of mine and has an official job with this here city, and he'll come right here if I call and tell him about all the trouble you're causing."

All of this scared the wits out of me, knowing Val would come but not for the reasons Louis thought. Val didn't know where I was spending my time all those days, but if Louis hadn't shut up, he would have known sooner, as one word brought on another and the bartender, too, threatened to call Val. I was in enough trouble with Val and I was sure Louis wasn't in very prize standing either, after that day at the carnival. Fearing that Val may have already been called and would walk in any minute, I visioned that Louis wouldn't be the only one thrown out. It was time for a conference with Lucy. After talking the situation over, Lucy and I tried futilely to persuade Louis to come home with us. We secretly planned to help him pass out at their little shack and then we could beat it back and finish our day at the bar.

Trying to drag that howling, kicking, dirty bulk of a man across the velvet carpet was nearly impossible for the two of us, and when we finally reached the door and let him get to his feet, he thumbed his nose at the bartender. We led him across the busy street, down a few blocks to the back door of their little shack, and began literally pouring the whiskey into his mouth to effect the final phase in our strategy. Even if we worked on him for an hour before he passed out, it

would surely be worth the effort and a relief to be rid
of that vile drunk for awhile.

We always knew when Louis was on his way "out"
as we'd so often heard his blowing off about the important job he used to have; how much money he had
made.   By that omen, we knew the hour of accom-
plishment was at hand, and we could soon return to
the bar and rave about what we *now had* or *could get*,
and not bore our listeners with faded memories as we
aspired to be the center of attraction.   There was sufficient time after our favor to Louis, for me to get
well saturated and leave the bar in time to reach home
before Val that evening.

But on leaving the bar I confused Val's hours and
mine, and decided to go by the shack with Lucy to
check on Louis before going to my own home.   (I
was always checking on somebody else — and not myself!)

We found that Louis had revived some though he
was sprawled half-off the cot on which we had placed
him.   He was eager to talk with Lucy and me, and as
we three sat drinking and talking the hours away, I
reminisced about the good ol' days in the South relat-
ing how much my family and I liked that Warren
family in our neighborhood. Louis seemed spellbound.
After his urging me to fill in with more detail, he
decided that we could be closely related as my descriptions fitted Louis' uncle on his father's side, for
sure.   Rolling off the filthy cot, he sighed and yawned
a few times, then brightly announced to his wife,
"Honey, let's get packed and head for the Dear ol'
Southland."

I gave them the Warren's address and also my
mother's address and phone number for in case they

had trouble finding their kinfolks my family could help them. I offered to help them pack their few possessions for the long trip back South to find their long-lost relatives. Within the hour the heavy old car pulled away, loaded and stacked with pasteboard boxes. A curtain of flowered oilcloth covered the back window as I sadly waved farewell.

(I sincerely hope that this displaced, unfortunate couple has found the road to sobriety as well as the road to the Southland.)

V

LIFE IN NEVADA

I drank continuously and steadily to ease my own tensions during the insipid divorce proceedings, but having decided that I had been tied down long enough as a married woman anyway, I made plans to return to freedom and my old haunts in Nevada. After a few days on the prowl, still pretending to be a stranger while hanging around anybody in the bars who would listen and feel sorry enough for me to buy me a drink, I was soon back in my old practices and traces. Although my recent ex-husband had withdrawn my use of his name, I was enjoying a residue of fine clothes. I could wear them in endless variety, fully aware that one could get many more free drinks if one were attractive-looking.

My hair was braided across my head and held in place with a jeweled comb. The comb matched my real silk, full-skirted dress and shantung high-heeled pumps, but neither helped to defer the inevitable arrest. I had hoped the police force would have changed since our last encounter. I soon discovered, with an inkling of embarrassment that, though there had been a few personnel changes, my illustrious record was still completely intact. Now, I was adding such charges as "nuisance in a bar", "drunk in a public place", and to top it all off, a "vagrancy" charge. In addition to my improved appearance, I derived a bit of satisfaction from giving them a new name and address, though in effect, it was no longer legal. Since my former husband had been spared paying a fine for me until now, I suggested to the little mustached judge that Val be wired for money with which to release me. In addition I suggested an allowance be included to cover the purchase of a bus ticket to Los Angeles. The funds arrived promptly and after meeting those expenses, there remained a few dollars with which to stock my little overnight bag with a fifth of whiskey.

Due to my partiality, I had to wait nearly two hours for the next Greyhound. While waiting I drank heavily from the bottle of whiskey, eventually falling asleep on the bench in the waiting room of the depot. Of course, this is absolutely prohibited regardless of the circumstances, so I awoke to find myself back in jail for supper with the pals to whom I had bade farewell just four hours earlier.

The officers detained me overnight purposely to sober up, and released me the next morning without further charges or fines. They suggested that I might be wise in moving on — preferably on the very next bus, regardless of its direction or destination. I didn't argue the suggestion, but having been in and out of nearly all the jails in California and Nevada, I longed for a town I'd not been in before — one where I wasn't immediately recognized as a vagrant and nuisance to society. Remittently, I realized that I was a nuisance to myself as well. I longed for another chance; another start toward shedding the burden of alcoholism. Just any quiet, peaceful little town that I might discover along the bus route would do. To initiate my renovation, I planned to taper my liquor consumption. I felt that eventually all would be well and right with my world. I had much to regret, much to lament, as the bus sped toward my undetermined destination.

After riding the ticket as far as the driver allowed, generously beyond the ticket's worth, I embarked upon my mission. As fate would have it, or by my aimless aspirations, I must have missed the quiet, peaceful little town for I alighted in the tremendous, intensely active depot of an obviously large city, still in Nevada.

With temptations of all sorts very prevalent to one so weak as I, all wasn't well long. Within a few short hours, during which time I had bummed more than a few drinks, I was again a drunk target for the police. Thoroughly saturated with alcohol, both inside and all over my clothes, I couldn't explain or remember anything beyond the first hour or so after my arrival. Following several hours' sleep in my cell, I awoke to learn that the judiciaries in this jail showed little patience with drunkards; due to the number of local offenses they deemed their efforts hopelessly wasted. Otherwise, the jail routine was typical for birds like myself, and after a week or so of familiar chores, such as scrubbing everything both vertical and horizontal, I would be released by the officers, almost eagerly. That contemptuous feeling was quite mutual, however.

About halfway through my eight-day sentence in jail, I was looking through those shining bars to the back end of the jail, catching the eye of a pitifully thin girl. She was bleak and haggard, robed in a blue denim sack dress issued by the jail matron. I had lost what had been a fine wardrobe within the past several weeks, but I was grateful that I didn't have to wear one of those horrid uniforms such as she was wearing. As I looked down at my soiled slacks and shirt, the girl called to me,

"Hey, Blondie, I may not have a change of clothes until somebody sends me some before kicking out time, but I have gotta place to go. I'll bet you ain't got no place to go when you get out, but if you wanna, you can go home with me. You can see our place from here, across over there. See?"

My eyes followed her pointed finger, and all I could do was credit the direction as a likely one to explore; the name she called the street didn't mean a thing to me. I was truly a stranger in town.

The invitation was music to my ears and I accepted. Later in the week I followed her, each of us being shabbily dressed alike as someone had sent her some slacks which were similar to mine. Her "place" was typical of skid row called "jail birds' paradise" by the townspeople. I certainly was not a fish out of water there.

An old iron grille balcony upstairs furnished a view of my entire world: the jail, the county court house, and the Greyhound bus station. The parlor was sparsely furnished with delapidated castoffs that blended perfectly with the ancient three-story rooming house and its occupants. The other tenants were girls of various extractions and descriptions, on the loose like myself — in and out of jail. When out of jail, the elderly couple in charge of the place gave the girls food and clothing donated by churches and the welfare department, helping all they could until the girls found jobs or left for other reasons. Bless their kindly hearts, that tiny hunchback yet motherly little woman who barely reached the elbows of her giant-size, jovial husband — they were trying almost in vain, as the tenants were surely to return to the roost.

In a day or two I had seen all of "jail birds' paradise" that even I could endure. Association with such an assortment and mixture of humanity was a new experience for me; one I cared not to repeat. Instead, I was ready for another jaunt into oblivion. I felt I was running like that greyhound painted on the side of my favorite form of transportation as I fled around the corner to the depot. (I wonder if they, the bus company, knew how partial to them this frequent passenger felt!) I was running, running fast; yet standing still. I was going nowhere fast.

I was dirty and tired from my exhausting visit in "jail birds' paradise" and my hair, though still braided, was a ruffled mess. I had taken time to wash and dry my slacks, so they were clean. I believe that had they shrunk another quarter of an inch, I wouldn't have been allowed on any kind of bus. I wanted to run for the bus station, but fearing the long strides would have a disastrous effect on my tight breeches, I proceeded with caution toward the ticket window. Tucking the ticket safely inside my blouse, I took a seat near the boarding platform, taking extra caution not to fall asleep in the waiting room of the station again; to somehow forestall my collapse until I was at last seated inside the bus. Sleeping peacefully is allowed on the bus (and in my case, mutually appreciated) and I looked forward to the rest. It would be of short duration, however, as my ticket, which required every dime I had, would carry me only about forty-five miles. I didn't know where I was going and cared less. But at least I was going somewhere, and anywhere was better than "paradise".

My deep, overdue sleep, was interrupted when a man tapped me on the shoulder and informed me that I had paid for only half of that double seat. I grumbled an apology and moved over as he requested, without looking up. He nudged me again after he was adjusted in his seat, and whispered:

"You look so tired, lady. Maybe a little drink would help your feelings. We can't let the bus driver see us, so hold your head way down to drink it or we'll be put off the bus."

I obliged heartily as he whispered in explanation that he had been forced off the previous bus. I couldn't imagine how the bus line could be so ungrateful as to put off another of their more patronizing passengers. I was slow to learn that drinking enroute is forbidden, and unfortunately for us, we became careless after a few turns each, spilled it all over the floor of the bus, and were dumped in the next town.

We were happy to find in that tiny crossroad-town a drinking haven which sheltered us from the blistering desert sun. We found an empty booth inside the torrid, drab little cafe in which we could continue drinking while waiting for the next bus through there. It was agreed that our being stranded in these circumstances certainly warranted introductions.

"I'm Leon Dooley," he said, "and I'm not such good company for young ladies, today. You see, I'm pretty hot under my collar because I got fired today — fired right on the spot — for drinking. I guess I deserved it, but I'm still mad as a hornet. Guess you noticed I'm pretty dirty, but like I say, I've just left work."

I expressed my deepest sympathy for him, confiding that I, too, had once lost a job for the same reason, though I didn't recollect ever being mad about it — just bewildered.

Leon conceded that perhaps he at least hadn't lost any money, and explained, "Well, the boss paid me up through today, so with my back-pay and my savings, I can get along all right. I have a little over $750, so I think I'll take off a few weeks to rest up and visit with my family — haven't seen them in six or eight months."

It had been an unusually long time since I had last contacted my own family. Having been able to call on Val for my needs for a comfortably long time eliminated my urgent collect calls home for financial assistance; that was a bed of roses compared to the bed of cactus now germinating.

As we sat across the table from one another, we spent several hours talking about ourselves. During that time Leon asked me to go with him to visit his folks. Thinking of that heavy pocketbook and his good drinking qualities, I agreed to go. I had never been in Arizona, and I could at least count on someone to foot my drinking costs for a while.

For the thousandth time he drawled with his own particular western style,

"I surely do like Southern girls, and it looks like I've found the cream of the crop. I could listen to you say 'yawl' the rest of my life, and I can hardly wait for my folks to meet you."

I hoped he couldn't read my mind. Considering our nearly liquified state it's a wonder I could think it, but I felt sure that my family wouldn't be pleased to meet him! However, the flattery improved, and a mutual appeal developed between us. By five o'clock that evening, we were standing in a quiet little chapel, before a Baptist minister who was clad appropriately in his cut-away suit. In this manner we were wed.

The minister and his prim little wife, who was summoned to stand as a witness, must not have been favorably impressed with our wedding attire. I was clad in slacks and soiled tennis shoes, and my new husband wore his khaki work clothes. We had excused ourselves previous to the ceremony in order to freshen up in rest rooms at the filling station. Leon didn't bother wasting the time to buy me a wedding ring, but he promised the minister that he would get me one later. What a surprise for my new in-laws!

The next day, after a night in the local motel, we resumed the interrupted bus trip, with the definite destination of Yuma to visit my new in-laws. The many miles of vast desert were spotted occasionally with Indian settlements of adobe huts still baking in the intense heat. Occasionally I saw an Indian mother carrying her precious cargo on her back, and it amused me when one papoose very loudly objected to his mother's bending to pick something off the ground.

We arrived at brother Ralph's home, a lovely, rambling ranch-style house on a country lot. Though we were quite obviously drunk, the delighted in-laws welcomed us, happy with the news that Leon had at last found a girl with whom to settle. They thought it was a wonderful day for everyone to celebrate but new problems and worries were actually arising for us all.

Ralph could have passed as Leon's twin, with his large frame and blondness. Susan, our sister-in-law, a most attractive blonde, worked in a downtown business office. Together, they were an exceptional couple, I thought. They seemed so devoted and well matched, blessed with a lovely home in the suburbs, complete with peace and contentment. They treated us like royalty on our honeymoon for the first four or five days, presuming that we were celebrating our wedding and not suspecting that they had two acute alcoholics on their hands. I soon realized that it was time to get at the business of being domestic, but it seemed strange to me that Leon did not share my enthusiasm. He continued his celebrating. Both Ralph and Susan were away working most of the day, leaving us alone in the house. I found it delightful while doing the cleaning and the cooking for Susan — but of course, it was the least the over-staying guests could do. I tried hard to model my marriage after Susan and Ralph's perfection, doing my best to make Leon happy even though he was most unreceptive.

I soon found it was the blind leading the blind when one day I had prepared a rather nice lunch especially for us honeymooners, and on finding there was no tea in the pantry, I had asked Leon to get some from a nearby store. I waited for him to return from his errand, and after several hours had passed I decided that he had gone to pick up a bottle of whiskey while out of the house, and had been detained by friends who hadn't seen him in months. The sober afternoon passed slowly, but when Ralph and Susan returned from work, I was quite eager to tell them about the day's happenings.

Ralph then told me that my husband had always been a problem, even as a child. He said they were willing to go to any length to help Leon get stabilized, and had hoped that his marriage to me would be decisive in their lives, too, in that Leon would settle down and quit roaming all over the country, returning to them only between sprees and jobs. Little did they know they had another problem on their hands — namely me. After assuring me that Leon was all right and would be back, Ralph remembered something, and said, "About a mile and a half down the road is a big Mexican family which has several little children, and Leon always visits with them. I know it's getting late and none of us has had any supper, but we'd better find Leon and put your mind at rest."

Leaving Susan behind to fix supper, Ralph and I drove through the dusk in search of Leon. Even in my quandary, I drank in the beautiful evening skyline of pinks and purples above the expanse of whiteness.

Soon I was to witness another stirring sight — Leon, centered in the midst of seven little Mexican children. They were all scurrying between two tremendous cast iron wash pots, rushing to get that mountain of wash on the lines before dark descended. Well, I thought, he does have one good streak in him to want to help that indigent family. When we pulled him away toward the car to come home with us, he handed the larger children some change from his pockets.

Conditions improved none whatever, but grew worse. I worried about the entire situation, discussing our problems with Leon as best I could, for I regretted the imposition on Ralph and Susan. If Leon was searching for love and understanding, he could have found it with me, for I tried with all my heart to get us on surer footing, but my fussing and mothering didn't do any good. Nothing I did helped, and the more I worried about the situation the more alcohol I consumed.

Finally when the savings were gone, the credit never had been extended in the first place, Leon decided to get a job. On the strength of his new found ambition, we left our in-laws and moved to an absolute shack. It was just a frame of a house and only half roofed, and was in the desert where the heat was surely hell. After we had hung our few possessions on nails in the house, Leon set out for his job on a rice plantation.

Leon worked until the first payday, and that pay was held at the office pending a discussion with the boss. It developed that he had "passed out" the previous night while irrigating one of the largest rice fields in that part of the country, causing half of the entire crop to be washed away. After getting his pay deducted by more than half Leon was committed to jail by the owner, leaving me alone again in that hull of a house.

I waited for him in that house, consoling myself with drinking profusely. When he returned it was to get me, and I followed him around everywhere he went, trying to keep up with him, and succeeding only in keeping up with his drinking. We were picked up together, but more often than not, separately. He was in jail; I was out. I was in jail; he was out. Week after week there was no "togetherness" anywhere except when we occasionally returned to Ralph's for a few hours.

We did everything together, except hop a freight train one night when he wanted to visit some more Arizona hobo-jungles. The only reason I missed the train was that he was too drunk to pull me up, and I was too drunk to pull my own weight. Leon was away for four days and I remained with Ralph and Susan, deciding that I had truly jumped from the frying pan into the fire. When he returned, only to face another drunk charge, I decided that he drank too

much, even for me. I knew I had stayed there long
enough anyway, so while he was still in jail, I left. I
figured I stood to gain another name and address out
of this marriage, and with those mementos I could find
new scenery once more.

Via my usual mode of transportation, I arrived in a
town not far enough away, and as much as I saw of it,
I thought it beautiful. The pleasant touring of local
bars was short lived, for three strange drinking pals
and I were invited to dine at the city jail that night
after being arrested on a public drunkeness charge.
It was in this jail that I finally received the delayed
wedding ring which my husband, Leon, had promised
the minister and me he would purchase. It was much
later for sure, and in a jail seventy-five miles away
from the one in which he was boarded. The vicious
circle continued — there seemed never to be a break
in it.

After we each were released from our separate jails,
he followed me. I had, in the meantime, rented a
little house-trailer on the outskirts of town, with financial help from my father, making a weak effort to
rehabilitate. Dad was delighted to hear of my plans,
and my promise to repay him this time as I had secured
a job in a small laundry at the check-out desk.

Sometimes people like us need to have company,
other than the steady, clinging companionship found
with a bottle of liquor. I bought fifty little baby
chickens to keep me company, and I built a shelter
for them — complete with a fence around it. I fed,
watered, tended and talked to them daily, and they
grew and grew as I watched over them so carefully.
We were like a family in which I, as "momma", hardily
thrived; until Leon at last found us. Before his de-

parture, the table had been turned upside down, food was scattered all over the trailer, curtains ripped from the windows, and as he left he turned all my chickens out to the wide open spaces. Again, it seemed that all my attempts at a better life and the little meaning I had found, had "flown the coop".

The landlord, a giant of a man and a retired sheriff who didn't deceive his title by any means, heard all the commotion and called the law officers. He helped haul Leon away to jail again, on a disorderly conduct charge. Upon appearing in court, the judge remembered that a wedding ring had been sent there a few weeks earlier. However, my husband, much to my further embarrassment, denied any knowledge of a wedding ring for any bride. Needless to say, another divorce suit followed, but the appearance of that wedding ring to that court scene is still a mystery.

VI

MY FIRST COMMITMENT

I had always wanted to see the big grape vineyards while in California and judging from all reports, I hoped I could get a job. Having heard that the wages were good, though seasonal, I worried little as I started down the highway again that late summer of 1947. Comfortably dressed in my traveling and working clothes, which you know by now to be slacks, I sought a job either picking grapes or working in one of the wineries.

Arriving at last in the orchard country, one of the largest grape producing sections in the world, I was awed by the beautiful, bountiful view; the gloss and the green looked almost artificial. Gigantic clusters of purple, all the eye could encompass, weighed heavily from verdant bending branches, at times touching and resting on the rich California soil beneath.

Alternately walking and hitching rides for many miles of highways directly through the vineyards, I finally stopped on the outskirts of a town to inquire at a bar for directions and information about job possibilities. I primarily concerned myself with obtaining some refreshment, feeling the effects of long hours of travel in the torrid sun. After I had settled in the privacy of a dimly lit booth in the back, near the gaily illuminated juke box, I kept the bartender busy answering my countless but almost pointless questions. He kept setting another drink in front of me (not that

I objected), and I was soon talking a mile a minute. He didn't suspect that my entire bankroll consisted of twenty-seven cents as he continued serving drinks, and as he responded to my chatter, I found the jolliest, best-natured bartender I had ever encountered — and the drunkest, for he evidently didn't want me to drink "alone".

As we sat there talking, the bartender began to think that I deserved lots of praise for being such a long way from home, and willing to work as common labor in a vineyard. As he kept putting feathers in my cap and drinks in my hand, I began to agree with him — maybe I was too pretty and too good to pick grapes.

In the meantime, a young man casually dressed in an army uniform bounced through the door like a ball, and in a double rush, he ordered, "Give me a double-header — and in a hurry. My father is waiting for me downtown, and I'm running late already."

With his sleeves meticulously rolled up, he reached for his drink across the bar, which the by-now very inebriated bartender was slowly preparing. When he served the drink to the handsome young man, the bartender inquired:

"How would you like to meet that pretty little girl with the braids over there in that booth? She's from the South, got the cutest way of talking you ever heard, and she's looking for a job in the vineyard, of all places."

Guzzling down his double-header, he looked over to me, revealing the deep-set, flashing eyes that caught my attention, and said as he sauntered over to me:

"Oh, you're too pretty to pick grapes — that's a nasty job, especially in this heat. I'm a crop duster for the vineyards and that's bad enough. But picking the durn things is worse. That's not for you!"

I didn't know a crop duster from a feather duster, but I sat there listening to all the local talk and accepting drink after drink. Dusk began to fall, and one doesn't pick grapes in the dark; so that was that, I thought. I wondered if the boy's father could still be waiting for him in town.

The younger man introduced himself as Wilbur Anderson, and began telling me of his army career; of having been a prisoner of war for a month. After another drink, he had been a prisoner for six months, and within a few additional drinks, he informed me that he had been a prisoner all during the war My heart was aching with sympathy for him and I felt sorrier for him than the bartender had for me much earlier in the evening. We three sat there for several more hours, analogizing and sympathizing with one another over numerous drinks, but suddenly Wilbur jumped up, and trying to be enthusiastic he said,

"You stay right here and wait — I'll be back in a little while. Don't you go away — because I will be right back."

I figured he couldn't hurry, remembering that perhaps his father was still waiting for him; but as I didn't have any plans, I would sit there and wait. Much to my amazement, he reappeared within a short while after all, and scampered over to the table. He handed me his Purple Heart, and with tears falling, he said:

"It's for you. I've saved it all this time just for you. And I've borrowed my father's car to take you wherever you want to go. Honey, you have no strings; neither do I. Let's go somewhere. Have you ever been in Nevada?"

I told him that I hadn't, but that I'd always wanted
to see some places there. He need not know just how
many places I'd already seen, though the sights were
limited mostly to jails, so I was silent on the entire
subject of Nevada.

Borrowing some money (a considerable amount)
from our blurry-eyed friend, the bartender, we headed
for Nevada in Wilbur's father's old car, and within a
few hours' time and acquaintance, we were married.
Having our honeymoon at the bartender's expense,
we went first class. We found a beautiful spot (in
a part of Nevada "new" to me) and reserved a cabin
beside a lake as blue as indigo, surrounded with sand
as white as snow. Enjoying the convenience of the
private swimming pool, we spent three leisurely days,
drinking and spending freely.

Paradise began ending as we heard over the radio
a police call requesting information on a stolen car,
described as ours; dark blue sedan with white sidewall
tires. My husband told me we were using his father's
car, and much to my relief, he quickly decided that
he had better let his father know that he was using
the car, his whereabouts, and announce a new wife,
too.

After reaching Mr. Anderson by telephone, we determined that I should be introduced as a girl he had
met in the Carolinas during his army hitch, and with
the immediate future cared for, we decided to take
one last but quick dip in the swimming pool before
leaving our lavish retreat. In Wilbur dived, all the
way to the bottom.

We managed to drive to Wilbur's hometown again,
which was back in the grape orchard section; Wilbur
with his head bleeding all over the car, and me drift-

ing in another world with "deetees" creeping on. I met my new in-laws in the hospital, to which we were taken and assigned adjoining rooms. Wilbur suffered a possible skull fracture, but within a few days we were each released and went to stay for a few additional days recuperation with his parents. The "borrowed" money entirely squandered during our honeymoon, Mr. Anderson had to pay the hospital bill, but he did it without a word, and accompanied us invalids to his home.

The Andersons were wonderful people and conscientious parents, active in their church and civic activities, but not too busy to feel compassion for their daughter-in-law during her sickness (neither of them realizing that I was in another world, suffering from alcoholism). They were unaware of the nature of my illness when we first met and I was under a siege of delirium tremens. While recuperating in our upstairs bedroom, Mrs. Anderson brought my meals on a tray, and whenever Wilbur could escape detection by his parents, he aided my recovery with a bottle of wine.

Mrs. Anderson was indeed a queenly woman. immaculate and regal in appearance, tall, blonde, and serene. Although her husband was amiable and undeniably worthy of his wife, he found some seething words a week later when Wilbur's crop dusting license was revoked permanently. He had been on "probation", and after several "stays", he was grounded absolutely. So it looked like we'd have to pick grapes instead of dusting them after all.

During the ensuing months when we were employed in the fields, I tried with all my heart to be a responsible wife; but again came the same old story of blind leading the blind. I actually talked with

Wilbur about our excessive drinking, suggesting that we take just "one" at breakfast, "one" at noon, and only "two" in the evening, in the hope that we would get sober eventually. But that didn't work; perhaps the attempt was too feeble. Nevertheless, we continued our trek down the tragic road of alcoholism.

A grape picker eventually is invited to tour the enormous winery to see the production of wine from beginning to end, and each visitor is given a little sample of wine at the end of the exhibition to commemorate the tour. Nothing could have been more to the liking of two booze hounds like us; and we soon overworked our welcome. With grape season nearing its end, we hadn't saved a dime. We began to make a few plans as to what we could do, and soon learned that we had been excluded in somebody else's personal plans — those made by Mr. Anderson. He had evicted us.

As in another similar incident in my memory, Wilbur re-enlisted in the Army, and a divorce followed.

Seemingly, the only place for me was behind bars, for there I at least had plenty of time to evaluate my predicament. I wondered sometimes if I was on the verge of losing my mind. One jail physician warned me that I had consumed about all the alcohol a human system could tolerate, and I knew how much I dreaded the resulting convulsions. In despair, I realized that about all I had to choose from was dying slowly or suicide, but in rational moments, I made more constructive plans.

I committed myself, for the first time, to the state institution for treatment, and I found I liked — and even enjoyed — being there, safe, sober, and sensible.

I was especially happy with the kitchen privileges I received, and I prepared meals for the hospital nurses. From the kitchen window I often scanned the beautiful grounds of the institution, dotted with other large buildings for different types of treatment and patients. As I was on the "Alcoholic List", I was given ground privileges after thirty days. During this time I enjoyed dances and recent movies sponsored by the hospital. But all was not devoted to amusement and entertainment, for when I was not employed in the kitchen, I helped with the mentally ill patients and their physical needs. For the first time in many, many months I felt a sense of human responsibility and personal contentment too satisfying to fully describe. My parents had no earthly idea where I was, but at least they were spared the collect calls urgently relaying my pleas for financial assistance.

My new-found worth was short-lived, as I was out into the open again after ninety days, undecided, without plans, and unable to help myself. Wearing the change of clothes that a nurse had given me upon discharge, I set out for the nearest main highway to put my thumb back into practice. Prompted by impulse I felt a desire to see the girls at Paradise again, only a few miles away. That distance was behind me in almost no time, for the driver of a long trailer truck, loaded with pipe, heeded my first twist of the ole thumb. Almost before I realized it, the driver had stopped at the front door of Paradise, and time had passed so swiftly that I had inadvertently spared the gentleman the wailings of a mistreated daughter. After wiring my father for grocery money, I went inside to pay the girls a visit, only to find that some of the girls had gone on; some were then in the state institution, and some were back in jail. Nothing had really changed; not even I.

It happened that my visit was cut short there, unintentionally. I fell during a stupor and suffered a broken shoulder, skinned face and bruises. While in the local hospital, my father contacted the attending physician to inquire if I could possibly have pneumonia again, for upon the latest request for money, he was at last doubting my recurring illnesses and desperate circumstances. But upon conferring with the doctor, funds were received to cover the costs of X-rays and the cast, which extended from the shoulder down to my elbow. Fortunately, all this happened to my left arm and not my drinking one, but I did find it difficult to manage all my parcels and effects.

With such a heavy cast and my usual encumbrances, it would be difficult to hitch-hike all the way to Los Angeles to stay with Pat. The first thing I deemed necessary was to wire for money again, and it was Mother's time to receive the call and solicitation. By alternating the requests, I knew that neither of my parents would be suspicious and compare notes, figuring that they were continuing their twice-annual visits. But this time Western Union somehow got its wires crossed, or my name incorrect (though at this point I wasn't positive of my own name, either). The expected money didn't arrive, or was too slow for my impatient desire to be on my way to Los Angeles. Hitch-hiking after all, I started out with only a few dollars, to arrive late at night and exhausted; but too late an hour to disturb Pat and the family.

Having long ago learned that one could check into a hotel if equipped with even just a small bag and be trusted to pay upon departure, I checked into one of the oldest hotels in Los Angeles, very accommodatingly near the bus station (in case a sudden traveling notion entered my mind). The little piece of luggage had become almost as important in my wanderings as the bottle of liquor with which I escaped. I had planned to walk out of the hotel, leaving the little bag behind and the bill unpaid; but instead, I was carried out on a stretcher to an awaiting ambulance, suffering with delirium tremens, screaming, kicking and otherwise disturbing the other hotel guests, no doubt.

The police officers accompanying the ambulance took me to the great General Hospital of Los Angeles, where I found help and understanding that I shall never forget. Writhing in that miserable cast which had become disgustingly filthy, being insane with fright and disease, I somehow understood the answers to questions I muttered concerning my being there. I was told the terrifying truths that I already suspected — my life was at stake.

A few days later when I had made miraculous progress, a gentleman with a most ethereal face appeared at my bedside to visit with me. I noticed his clear eyes and genuine smile as he looked down at me and introduced himself as the Reverend Luther Little, affiliated with the Christian Church. He gave me a pamphlet about The Book of John to read when I was feeling better, but for the next few days I wondered how he had gotten his information about my connection with the Christian Church during my early youth in the South. (I'd like to insert at this point that this same minister is still actively engaged in God's Work and knows of my recovery from active alcoholism).

The Reverend Little arranged for a most gracious and understanding middle-aged lady to meet me upon my release from the hospital. I shall never forget the day she literally danced into the room, chatting gaily as she entered to find me ready and waiting, but lying across the bed. She talked so fast that I could hardly catch a word she said, and as she nodded to emphasize a particular phrase, the flimsy feather atop her big black straw hat flopped about, much to my amusement. In rapid fire, she told me all about herself before we ever left the hospital. I sympathized with her nervousness, worries and family problems; now she had all of my problems. She was fascinating yet frivolous, and I was doubtful of her best intentions, not convinced that I should leave there with her. Little did I anticipate that I was going to the home of a most wonderful, compassionate woman, dedicated to helping each and everyone caught in a disease like mine.

VII

MOM'S HAVEN

It would be unfair to beat around the bush in describing her, for she is known and endeared to thousands in the Los Angeles area and surely hundreds across the nation, as "Mom" Turpin. She is now seventy-two years old, residing with her daughter and son-in-law in Whittier, California. It has been my good fortune to have Mom visit me twice in recent years, and she has been a great source of encouragement toward putting my thoughts into print.

Mom, as a marvelous model of maternity, was graying but aging beautifully the crucial day I was taken into her home and influence. Pop, her husband, who has since passed away, was a retired railroad engineer, and one could readily enjoy his exceptional sense of humor just by speaking to him while he sat in his usual spot — his comfortable lounge chair from which a cloud of pipe smoke always arose. Their home in one of Los Angeles' nicest neighborhoods was a large brownish-colored house. Across the front there extended an inviting porch which was filled with several old-fashioned flower pots, hanging baskets overflowing with trailing vines of all sorts, and the comfortable porch furnishings. The furnishings included many rocking chairs and a long leather-covered glider, which was a favorite recline of everyone. Inside, a certain end of the living room sofa was reserved for Mom, and as industrious as she was, she never just sat but always utilized her time mending, knitting or crocheting; though her daily retreat there with her Bible reading came first. Pop's recliner and ottoman was enviably near Mom's end of the sofa where he could extract from her long, busy day, just a little while in her inspiring company.

My general disreputable appearance didn't make any difference to Mom — she still welcomed me into her home with open arms. Within the first hour or so, she had provided me with a warm bath, fresh clothes and dinner, in a most royal manner. Thereafter, we would often enjoy long talks, sometimes until the wee hours of the morning, discussing her church work and other activities, and I would recall my happy years as an active young churchwoman, the sad years that followed, and my vague plans for the future. However, despite the perfect environment and conducive atmosphere, I soon found myself looking forward to the day a few weeks hence when the cast would be removed, enabling me to carry my bag, bottle and belongings, and leave.

As though Mom detected what I was thinking, she encouraged me to remember my early life and ambitions, promising me that I could resume those plans and be of real service to humanity. She foresaw really wonderful things coming my way if I could stop one thing — Drinking. I knew by her choice of words and the calming tone of her voice that she wanted to help me — with all her heart.

Again dismissing the ideal from my thoughts, I wondered how she managed to provide for me and that constant stream of girls coming to and going from her house. She never failed to accommodate a single one, though she often indicated jokingly that she may have to hang a couple of them on nails. There was always room for one more at her ample table, and there was always time and an open heart to anyone who wanted time with her; but never a word of complaint came from the lips of this angelic woman that I, too, began to call Mom in the dearest sense.

I had never known a person so unselfish, unrelenting; so kindly and dedicated. If any of the many girls went astray or even landed in jail, Mom retrieved her. She supplied every physical need and with staunch moral support she encouraged and never criticized as she waited, helped and hoped that we would regain purposeful places in the world.

As Mom was knitting a brown sweater one day, she asked without looking over the top of her glasses as she usually did when she rested, if I would attend a club meeting with her, the purpose of which she had described to me several times during our long heart-to-heart sessions. I had already recalled having heard of this organization of Mom's before, from the couple and lady who visited me in that little shack in Stockton, and curiosity was mounting. I consented to go only to satisfy that curiosity, and I was amazed to see so many smiling, gay and sober people, evidently all members of the club that had no bright-colored lights, soft music or reckless dancing. I decided either I was losing my mind, or these people were. Didn't they know what they were missing?

I left the meeting a confused girl and returned home with Mom. As strange as things seemed to me there, I thought I may as well stay a while longer — it's far better than standing on the hot highways or sitting forlorn in jail. I expected her to suggest my going out and getting myself a job soon, and I had my answer ready — I had no coat. With the realization that this generous soul would have given me hers if I needed it, I guiltily decided to be honest and make the approach concerning a job.

Mom concluded our discussion by saying, "Your shoulder and arm are not yet strong enough to use as needed with any type job, so I suggest that you take it easy for awhile longer; but perhaps you can help me a little bit with the housework, doing the light things that you are able to do."

I found it fascinating to help, and kept busy shining furniture, dusting in remote corners, etc., thinking it quite possible to find a hidden treasure in the liquid form somewhere. Occasionally, I would discover a bottle someone had hidden away for a rainy day, much to my delight. All this sort of activity was not doing light housework by any means, but I felt displaced and displeased.

As days passed my thinking began to clear in some respects, due greatly to Mom's gentle counselling, yet I remained confused. I couldn't understand the generosity of this fine woman, or how she managed to do the dozens of chores to which she was so enthralled. It seemed almost a waste to lavish her time and efforts so relentlessly on hopeless alcoholics like myself, but at least I sensed the seriousness of my condition.

I suddenly slackened in my job of helping Mom with the housework, and not realizing the basis, I ravenously craved a drink. The desire hit my mind like a cyclone, and I was soon back on the run trying to outsmart everybody and smuggle in a bottle.

Those jeopardizing thoughts prevailed again and it was impossible for me to keep up with my contraband jobs that reaped only havoc, and keep up with the household chores at the same time. Upon comparing my many days of wandering aimlessly, hitchhiking and drinking and invariably landing either in jail or a hospital, to this bewildering way of life with Mom, I was nevertheless, anxious to be out and left to my own vices once more. Yet, I wanted to understand the mechanism of this haven to which I'd come. My mind seemed beyond sane reasoning; it was just plain warped I feared.

If I stayed my distrust caused me to be suspicious of someone wanting a favor from me, whether it be my precious bottle, money, or something else equally preposterous. If I left, I knew what I would be missing. With so many new friends, so many girls returning to say thanks for clothes, financial help or a job, I knew a wonderful spirit lived within this house.

I was soon asked by a couple, friends of Mom's who also belonged to her club, to come visit in their home several miles away, for a few weeks. Their only daughter had recently married and they were lonely without her, it seemed, and I was given her bedroom to use. Laden with ruffles — the curtains, bedspread, chairs and vanity — all matching in floral patterned chintz, I felt like a Hollywood star as I gazed dreamily into the tremendous mirror above the vanity table. I had never seen such a lavishly decorated bedroom, and it was evident the Fonders were devoted to their daughter and were excruciatingly lonely without her. Mrs. Fonder, one of the sweetest women I had met, suffered miserably with asthma attacks, and except on those occasions, she gave attention to me, causing me to feel a longing for my own mother who was so far away.

Most members of the club are sincerely intent in

remaining sober, but Mr. Fonder, a balding but quite amiable gentleman, was still a practicing alcoholic — much like myself, in a way. He had many more valuable household and personal items to sell in order to buy whiskey (if necessary) than I ever had. And the pantry was stocked to the ceiling in preparation for the day that Mrs. Fonder carried out her threat to leave him; he was looking ahead to the day when he wouldn't have strength, time or money to leave the house for groceries.

The Fonders had heard favorable comments on real Southern cooking and soon asked me to prepare a few special dishes for them. I didn't put much care or effort into those meals, and I'm sure they were sadly disappointed in my renditions.

Enroute to their most attractive home, I noticed a liquor store around the corner from their house, to which a police watch had been assigned. Not only were they anticipating Mr. Fonder, but they had been alerted to expect me, too. I wandered toward the store quite casually, to be surprised by the awaiting officers.

I had been in many a courtroom but this instance will always remain vivid in my memory, as it was the occasion of my being in the "line up", and I was "number three" to be called to the stand to plead guilty. I felt so sorry for the rest of the bunch as they stepped before the stern judge — some had been beaten up, many carried two black eyes and others only one; many had bad cases of shakes like myself. The majority of the men had beards an inch long, and some of them blamed their wives for their drinking; and vice versa. Some of them could hardly hobble to the stand to tell the judge whom they blamed, but regardless of their excuses, the judge announced that he would not tolerate any of us any longer.

The court sentenced me to ten days, following which Mom came to the jail to meet me. I told her that there was entirely too much drinking at the Fonders, and that I had found it imperative to leave. With me in tow, Mom returned home, never uttering a word of reprimand, but as soon as the sun set, I left.

I thought that I would never see my second husband again, but after one and a half years, our paths crossed again, quite intentionally. I caught the red street car to the little town not far from Los Angeles to pay him a visit. Briefly within the city offices I let him know in no uncertain terms what I thought of him and all the other Californians who had mistreated me; just an innocent visitor to their lovely, but heartless, state. And having said my piece, I left, frantic to find the nearest bar. As usual, after a few drinks, that escapade netted me another stint in jail; but I was released at kicking-out time from that tiny jail, which had only one cell that was barely large enough to contain me, before Val came to work for the day. Then, I was well on my way back to Los Angeles. My vehicle was a lettuce truck, on the back of which I was relegated as the driver had picked up another drunk before me. I could see through the back window that the other rider was rapidly emptying his bottle while I perched like a jealous rabbit on top of all that lettuce.

Even though the driver was running four hours behind schedule, he went up and down the street on which I believed the Fonder's house to be, until at last I found it. As I groped up the sidewalk, I re-

membered from several years back when I was in the
Stockton State Institution that the end of my road
was near, and in agony I foresaw the possibility that
I could spend the rest of my life in an asylum. Here
I was at their doorstep again, wanting and needing
help, and wanting to follow the advice of the club
members.

Taking their advice, I accepted their offer to drive
me to another institution near Los Angeles where I
planned knowingly to commit myself as an alcoholic,
but I insisted that the Fonders allow me time enough
to write Mother.

Many months had passed since I had last contacted
my family, even on my imaginary medical emergencies, and I decided that before I committed myself to
an institution, perhaps for life, I wanted to unload
my misgivings toward them in one, long, deliberate
letter instead of a hurried telephone call. The letter
would surely wake them up to realize belatedly that
they were the cause of my downfall and the resulting
commitment. After several drinks, the letter was completed and underscored, and I felt very satisfied with
myself and the misguided epistle.

Ironically, it's certainly time to be committed for
life when one gets as helpless and hopeless as I was
after so many years of alcoholic rule. With such fore-
sight, I knew I wouldn't like the necessary treatment
at the institution, and the ward confinement was
misery personified. After three weeks of yielding to
a wheelchair and depending upon another recuperating alcoholic to push me around I regained some
of my equilibrium and managed to walk, though falter-
ing from chair to chair. I was soon looking forward
to ground privileges as allowed after thirty days prog-

ress and good behavior, plotting secretly my way to the hospital store.

Suddenly the hospital building began shaking, beds and chairs began rolling around, and everyone was screaming in hysteria. Doors slammed and locked, and I knew the world was coming to an end as I watched nearby buildings sway from the window near which I was trying to stand. Within seconds we were all evacuated to the outside, though none of us felt much safer outside than inside. It was then that the Bakersfield and Los Angeles areas were shattered and shuddered by an earthquake. A few days later I shattered the progress I had made in the hospital — again.

With two other girls I'd met at the movies and dances sponsored by the hospital, we planned our escape. Ground privileges were to our advantage, so it was a simple matter just to walk off the grounds casually, and then hurry for distance once off the premises. We were dressed in hospital-issue cotton print dresses and out in public, we couldn't be identified as escaped patients. Wearing low-heel walking shoes, we weren't uncomfortably hampered as we scampered out of sight.

One of my runaway buddies was quite a character in her own right; though frail and pathetically gaunt, she wasn't afraid of the devil himself. "Skinny", the appropriate nickname by which she always answered, could walk faster than those horses could run at the tracks and since she was in a hurry that particular day, I had to run steadily to keep up with her. Our little black-eyed Mexican friend, "Cortez", was just too short and dumpy to keep up with me, much less "Skinny", but finally, one by one, we reached a bar some dozen or so blocks away.

We collapsed in a booth just long enough to get our thirst quenched, but of course that required several drinks each. When we were ready to move on, we left the little Mexican member of our trio as she had found it difficult to keep up in the first place and had decided to return to the hospital after her fling. As she was being taken back to the hospital, possibly, we two were making our way to Capistrano, the famous little mission to which swallows return.

Always striving to get ahead of everybody and do everything in my own time, and even the season in this case, we found the park completely void of any other living creature. The waterfall there typified our tears when we found no swallows; only exhaustion and pain. Disappointed with only a bird's-eye view of the mission, we wandered aimlessly down the busy highway.

Somehow in my near delirium, I remembered a particular doctor at the hospital and decided to call him by phone. On the pretense of being a relative calling, I reached the very busy doctor and listened to him give us instructions to stay where we were until he dispatched a state car to return us to the hospital. Not realizing how long it would require a car to drive the forty miles, we decided we had waited long enough after too short awhile, and trudged on. By then the entire area had been alerted for us, as is usual when patients leave the hospital grounds without authority; and three days later we were detained at the psychopathic division in San Diego, to await transportation back to the institution in Los Angeles.

Nurses in stiff white uniforms and pert caps warmly and sympathetically greeted "Skinny" and me when we entered the psycho-ward. They immediately began their concentrated procedure to sober us. Everything everywhere was spotlessly clean, especially in the kitchen to which "Skinny" and I were assigned detail, washing trays and dishes side by side, managing to snitch a little extra food to pad our long-empty stomachs.

I noticed many mentally ill persons, both old and young, and as I looked at them I longed in my heart to say or do something to help them. My own mental faculties were somewhat weakened, but I wondered why I couldn't get sober and stay sober. I wanted to work possibly in a hospital such as this or in some other way give of my life something good to others so helpless; never admitting how incapacitated I was myself. Hoping to find myself at last, I actually regretted leaving that psycho-hospital when our state escort arrived to take us back to Los Angeles.

To go into complete detail about my experiences in the Los Angeles institution for the next six months would be far too lengthy, and much was repetitious of my many former experiences in treatment for alcoholism. Within a short while, (which seemed like an eternity) the pains left my nearly deformed legs and I soon began to actually enjoy my detention to a rewarding extent. With the responsibilities I was to assume working with some of the staff and many of the patients there was much mutual benefit.

I experienced quite an awakening when I first began detail in a ward of elderly people. There before me were scores of people, who perhaps through their own regrettable lack of stamina or an accidental fault of society or heredity were now ostracized from the world. Each individual was a mystery case to me into which I had no intention or talent to probe, but they had been long forgotten by their families and loved ones. I certainly hoped they weren't as sad for themselves as I was for them. Though I didn't have any real material things to share with them, other than a few pieces of candy occasionally, they began to call me their "little fairy godmother". I think they enjoyed singing around the old piano as I played songs and hymns familiar to them, and amazingly familiar to me. As I too, reminisced, I longed to see my mother and family, to whom I had not written in months; I promised myself a visit with them when I was free and well again.

Mom Turpin came regularly on visiting days, usually bringing some of our club friends along to visit with me, also. I looked forward to seeing Mom's radiant smile when she came, and though she must have been disappointed many times on hearing of my erratic behavior, she must have purposely avoided showing it. Thoughtfully, Mom Turpin had written my family in the meantime as to my confinement in the institution again. Regardless of their reaction to the news, at least they knew they wouldn't be getting collect telephone calls at odd hours every other week or so; they must have felt some relief for my safety, anyway. The more I thought of them all, the more eager I was to go home.

Freedom was granted and my discharge followed after a long talk with several of the doctors, and they joined with the many nurses and attendants who had become true friends, in wishing me a well and happy future. I owe so many of these specially trained personnel so much, and delighting in their praise of my progress, I returned to Mom's house as if magnetized.

As a little lost girl returning home, I was lovingly

welcomed with open arms — and the arms had to open a bit wider. Friendship with one of the hospital kitchen employees had reaped me extra helpings of my favorite dishes, which had netted twelve extra pounds on my bones. Mom had brought me a dress, donated by her church, but it had to be returned for a larger size!

Mom was still wonderful Mom, hurrying about her big house tending to her many half-sick guests and managing all the consequential chores of providing them with food, clothing and understanding, the latter coming easily and naturally. I was happy that I was responding to her faith in me and with some faith and confidence in myself, I applied for a job in a sanatorium for elderly people. I counted on Mom as a reference and, having acquired some practical experience while working and recovering in the institution, was thereby provided with another job.

I was interviewed by the Mexican lady who, as a registered nurse, operated the sanatorium. I found her to be more than typically congenial and sympathetic with me, and she seemed to understand my past record and lack of many references. Mom provided me with a white uniform and I was eager to start work, if just to push the medication cart around behind a nurse as I had often done before. After first spending a few nights in a small storeroom upstairs, I was invited to use the small wardrobe closet (it was plenty of room for my stock) and the narrow cot, until I could find a place to live near the sanatorium, which proved to be an inconvienient distance from Mom's house.

The private sanatorium accommodated approximately thirty-five patients, most of whom were bed-

ridden or completely helpless. Several were retired
doctors from the Los Angeles area, and were most
interesting to talk with during my leisure time. I was
enraptured by stories of old Los Angeles at a time
when the doctors had made their sick calls in horse-
drawn buggies, taking hours to travel through towns
over rough roads, and to outlying districts where there
may have been only a foot path.

After several months of working in the sanatorium,
though absorbed in my satisfying duties, my fortitude
weakened occasionally, but through the understanding
of the most considerate supervisor, I was allowed to
remain on the job. With renewed determination for
abstinence I started saving my money, and after three
months (the longest sober period in nine years) I was
both physically and financially ready for my long-
planned trip home to see my family. I had so much
to tell them, and I longed to hear their voices and
learn what had been happening at home.

With luggage borrowed from Mom, filled with
clothes she had helped me accumulate (mostly through
donations from her church society) I boarded the
Greyhound Bus in Los Angeles. Much about the
long over-land trip was novel — I was completely
sober, my baggage was filled with garments only;
and I actually went across all of Texas without getting thrown off the bus for breaking the standard rule
against drinking on board.

I hadn't written or even called any of the family of
my pending visit home, and it must have been a real
surprise to Brother Red when I called from the depot.
I shall never forget his words as he called out,

"Oh! Momma, it's Sister — and she sounds sober!"

Reliving old times and expounding heavily upon the

places I'd been, the sights I'd seen, the big things I'd done, and the substantial jobs I'd had, I obviously remained the same old phony and liar they remembered, but I noticed various changes in the family scene, both basically and distantly.

Dad broke his strict schedule of visiting days and came to see me, evidently pleased with my appearance, for there was no scolding for my errant behavior from him or Mother. My father bore the news that Pat, Pauline and the children had moved back South with Val's financial assistance, sometime during my six months' confinement in the Los Angeles institution; and lived some one hundred and fifty miles further North. Pat's drinking had been continuous despite his happy homecoming, and he had died just a few weeks following the transfer; reportedly, from a heart attack. In those days that diagnosis was preferred over "alcoholism".

On being told of Shirley's successful career overseas with the Government, elaborately described, I noted that I had for four years traveled extensively, too; though still somewhat envious of her good fortune.

When Polly came home to introduce her new husband to me, I was delighted with my little sister's choice, and wished them much happiness for the future but maintained complete reticence as to my own marital attempts and failures. Buck was home on furlough and though Dad's health was failing, he rejoiced in Buck's ambition and progress, and contributed all he could to foster Buck's aspiration to study law after his discharge. Mother relished every moment of having us all, except for Shirley, home for a happy, though brief, reunion.

After a few days visiting and revisiting, I remembered the liquor store I had frequently visited many years ago, and allowed my curiosity to take me inside to inquire of my bartender-friend's health and habits. The next day, after a discussion of the rise and fall of prices, and the pros and cons of miniature flavor, I relented and purchased a pint. My family had said long years ago that they would like so much to see me sober just one more time; well — they had, now. I had been sober long enough.

After nearly a week of slipping out at night, ashamed for Mother's neighbors to see me and daring them to recognize me after so long anyway, I was ready to move on, as soon as possible. I had been inconvenienced here long enough, whereas in California I didn't find so much distance between me and the nearest liquor store; and I certainly didn't hide to drink it. Leaving my family wondering when and if they would ever see me again, I boarded the bus West, well supplied with two full fifths of whiskey.

With Texas miraculously behind me, considering my parcels, I gave my seat on the bus to a little dark Mexican lady who flagged the bus from the burning highway in Arizona. She held on her lap a chicken caged in a wire box, and she looked up as I resumed singing, quite flatly, with a man who had accompanied me for miles playing his Jew's harp. Moved by all that melody, the little chicken soon chimed in with her cackling. But she had laid an egg, and now we were a jubilant trio.

VIII

DOWN MEXICO WAY

My family heard of me some sooner than they expected perhaps, and they may not have been too shaken when the return address showed first one hospital or institution and then another for the next three months, in or around Los Angeles. Circumstances had returned to the old pattern, but at least we were corresponding. Again committed to a psychoward after another long seige of constant drinking, I later regained consciousness enough to realize that I had sunk to a new low. I feared that I was surely losing what little mind I may have left. Fighting insanity, I rallied enough to be asked to be the housekeeper for one of the women doctors whose home was on the hospital grounds. She displayed much sympathy and understanding when I repeatedly lost sight of my goal, but after fifteen months of additional incursions, the hospital administrators presented me with a discharge. On the back of the form was written "N.F.B.N.", which I learned meant, "No Further Benefit Necessary". I could no longer be admitted to that state's institutions for help — I was being termed a hopeless alcoholic. I thought that if I was ever in such a shape again, they wouldn't admit me.

Agreeing with the ultimatum that my case was hopeless, anyway, I continued to drink heavily, constantly and shamelessly. Meanwhile, however, I continued attending those club meetings with Mom and her crowd, still looking for the hidden meaning of their discussions. At such a meeting one night I suddenly thought of my father, and realizing that I hadn't written to him in several months, I scratched off a note and included in the envelope some of the club literature that was readily available, explaining that I was attending the meetings but not understanding or anticipating what could come of it.

In less than thirty minutes after Father received my letter, he was at his typewriter with his reply. He was very ill and hadn't worked in many months he said, and often prayed for me to change my foolish way of living. He gave a brief summary of the family news, and closed with another fervent plea for my sake. I hold his last letter to me as one of my dearest possessions, as it contributes to my ultimate recovery.

While attending meetings with Mom regularly, I attempted to get through the long days and endless nights with just a few drinks instead of a few bottles; a method hopefully termed "tapering off". Needless to say, the procedure didn't work for me, and I soon requested, on Mom's and a doctor's advice, admission to the hospital for another three month period; and upon that release further treatment was invariably required — again and again.

During one of the treatment periods I received the heartbreaking message that my beloved father had passed away. Sorrowful that I had not seen him in so many months, and unable to attend his funeral, I was miserable with grief. My name, and a prayer that I would soon be all right were among the last words he spoke from his deathbed, I later learned from the family. And he wired his few remaining dollars to me, in care of Mom Turpin. In only ten more days I would have been released from the hospital, but those then-remaining days of treatment seemed an eternity, for which I could not wait. I felt I had every reason to leave with or without permission, considering the circumstances.

Instead of contacting my family upon leaving the institution, I wandered about for a day, long enough to entangle myself in such a jam that I was somewhat outdone with myself when I finally came to my senses. How had I gotten to Mexico, and how could I explain or question all these people who just stared at me in bewilderment? I had always thought myself too smart to get trapped, yet I was cornered in a foreign land. Despite all my plainly spoken English and simple sign language, the Mexican jailers did nothing but provide nerve pills during the day. I heartily recommend taking an interpreter to Mexico, for all purposes.

Being from the States, I was far from mistreated, I hasten to say; but I regretfully add that if ever there was a hell on earth, it was in that filthy Mexican jail.

I had been accustomed to cleaning bars, commodes, etc., but a life sentence wouldn't have been long enough to get that place halfway sanitary. On the bars, between the bars, on the floor, walls, on the bed and under it, was a coagulation of chewing gum and assorted filth, utterly indescribable. It was in that jail that my long hair had its first cut in many a year, and not by my choice; but it had become matted with chewing gum, vermin and vomit overnight and there was no alternative but to lop it off. My breath vile with odor, my clothes drenched with emetic and vomit from the all-night seige, and my numbed senses reeling, I was experiencing a hell in reality.

Just as delirium tremens reached their peak, attendants from the local hospital arrived to transfer me to the infirmary, escorted by badge bedecked police officers. On admittance to the hospital, which was thankfully much cleaner than jail, I noticed almost immediately that even there the potent national drink, Tequila, seemed to flow like water. The nurses, wearing bright red uniforms instead of our customary white ones, literally poured the drink into me, and I couldn't decide whether the purpose was to bring me to or put me out. Despite all they did for me for three anxious days, I responded none as they worked constantly with me, but became weaker instead, and despondently prayed to die. I could not even see, and was ready to give up.

During a hazy seige several days after my reception, I lifted my fatigued eyes to see a very lovely person standing beside my bed, looking down at me. The fair-faced white haired lady handed me a little bouquet of waxed flowers, and explained that the Mexican police department had asked her to come to me, and she was eager to do whatever she could to help. The sound of her voice was music, and she was a perfect example of my childhood ambitions, a missionary.

Following her check to see if I was bruised or hurt, I learned that I had been involved in an automobile accident on the border. I wondered how I happened to be in a car in the first place, but it did account for my hospitalization in Mexico. A woman was fatally injured in the wreck, and I recalled that long ago night when my landlady in Stockton assured me that the Lord and all His angels were watching over me. I was fortunate to be alive, though a few hours earier I had prayed for mortal release.

After the missionary contacted Mom in Los Angeles, I was soon on my way to the border, arrangements having been made for the San Diego police to make connections with my Mexican escort. From the border, my destination was the San Diego psycho-ward again, and between the glucose feedings night and day and various other injections, I realized that there hadn't been a real finality to the "N.F.B.N." notation in my records after all. I would be able to go to institutions repeatedly for the rest of my life, apparently, and there were hospitals, institutions and psycho-wards from coast to coast that I hadn't even tried yet. I had little to worry about — the future would take care of itself. I could pull through every time.

Able to travel a little better, I was again transferred, to the State Hospital, whereupon I was greeted by most of my runaway pals. Their last discharges had read just like mine. Treatment would never be denied.

After tottering around from chair to chair for a few weeks, I regained strength enough to go to work again within the hospital. I was detailed to the ward of elderly people as before, and I tried and succeeded in displaying commendable patience as I dealt with them. Together with other inmates, I waxed floors, helped the nurses and patients undergoing shock treatments, fed the mentally ill, and kept constantly busy doing something constructive.

Mom Turpin soon learned of my return to the Los Angeles hospital, but as she didn't drive a car, it appeared that I wouldn't get to see her often. But thanks to two special friends who belonged to the club, they saw to it that Mom visited me often.

One of the ladies was from a small town in the South not too far from my own hometown; so we had much in common, except that she had been sober for some ten or twelve years, and I had yet to master one. I used to say to myself — If that Southerner can do it, I can, too. With her overwhelming personality and lively smile, I always welcomed her. Her name, "Dollie", represents all the lovely things she was and still is.

Dora, Dollie's close friend and ally, was a great consolation to me on their visits as she confided that she, too, was still a victim of alcoholism and had had a tragic life because of it.

When we three were sitting on a bench on the hospital grounds one day, Dollie looked at me, laughing as usual, and said, "You could be one more Southerner to rise again."

How often did those words ring in my ears and heart as the years went by, and those two gals share a big part of my heart today whether or not they are aware of it.

For a change of scenery I often attended club meetings held within the compound, but I still derived little from the discussions on obtaining and retaining sobriety. The methods suggested seemed to have a remote chance for success, I thought.

I soon learned that my ground privileges had been withdrawn due to my past record, and after seventy-four days of being escorted to and from the ward in which I lived to those in which I worked, I asked Dr. Thorpe, a stern and strict disciplinarian, why I needed to be a virtual prisoner. Sitting behind her desk in her stiff white coat, and looking over her glasses at me, I was very resentful toward her when she said to me in a calm but emphatic way,

"My dear, we're trying to do all we can to help you in this State, but you don't seem to realize or appreciate it. Don't your remember my telling you, warning you, saying that if you didn't help yourself and permanently stop drinking, you could become permanently institutionalized — right here. You've just got to realize the seriousness of your condition."

Then to verify how often attempts had been made to help me, she opened the file cabinet and withdrew my records:

"Here is the file showing your past record in the State. Maybe if you look at it, you'll know why you aren't allowed ground privileges. We doubt that you can be trusted on the grounds, to stay here and receive all the help we can offer, the entire treatment which you badly need."

The folder was thicker than this book, and the confinements could be condensed numerically to this:

Psycho-wards	11 times
State Hospitals	8 times
	(3 month periods)
General and County Hospitals	7 times
Various Jails	21 times

I called Dr. Thorpe's hand when she showed me an entry which included San Francisco among the hospitals to which I had been confined, however, as I jumped up and said:

"I've never been anywhere near San Francisco in my life, and I don't like being accused of something I didn't do. I've done enough, I'll admit, but that entry is a big mistake."

As if it made such a big difference! Until then I

must have never realized that a person's past records were retained like that; to live such a record down would be impossible.

Back to arguing with Dr. Thorpe, I felt I had done my part in penance to society and since I had been locked up for over three months, making good progress and working hard, I was getting a raw deal. She listened patiently as I verbally rebelled, but she made no concessions.

Many forms of entertainment were available to the recuperatives such as movies and square dances, and I was allowed to attend all the inside functions under close supervision. My usual partner for the square dancing was a big, red-faced Irishman named Vincent, who I thought, was a typical alcoholic. He had told the officials at the hospital that he was president of a railroad, and that he had been reprimanded for sending his crew home early one Friday.

Between dances Vincent and I would have time to talk about things on the outside — what was going on, what we'd do and where we'd go when we were released as did many other "couples". After much dancing and more association, we eventually began plans for getting married upon discharge to start life anew together. He professed to be a big property owner, having a beautiful beach home facing the Pacific, but what caught my attention most was the private beach included in the property, as this portion of the property seemed to be his share of the community property split after he divorced his wife for excessive drinking.

As time grew near for our releases (which were just several days apart) I noticed that Vincent began to worry about something. For the life of me, I couldn't see what he had to worry about for as owner of such valuable property in addition to his being a railroad official, what more did he want?

The women were dressed in brilliant new square dance dresses that had full, gathered skirts, with tiny puffed sleeves. These were furnished by the hospital to commemorate the last big, competitive square dance before our releases. I noticed Vincent had become almost silent and motionless.

"Why aren't you having a good time, too? Everyone else is having a ball. What's bothering you? You act so worried about something," I asked as he gave me a half-swing.

"Honey", he said, "I want you to know before it's too late that when the community property was settled, I let the beach property be put in her name as she was sick from drinking too much. However, as soon as we are married, I'll put all my fortunes in your name."

I hope others' plans materialized better than mine and were not as easily "railroaded" as I nearly was while day-dreaming. However, some unforeseen things *did* materialize, and many of us were bound to meet again at the admitting office — for further treatment.

When we were released at last, I took Vincent to meet Mom and to share our plans with her. As we courted, we used Mom's place as a nest to roost in, where every week Vincent would pass out on her porch glider. Feeling sorry for him out there in the cold, Mom's considerate husband would cover him with a dusty old canvas. You know, there's no greater love than one of us has for another. Similar to a cow having wallowed in hay, lint and dust covered what hair he had left and he looked far more like the president of a cotton gin than a railroad.

Eventually Mom was forced to call the police, and when the judge sentenced Vincent to thirty days in jail, that delayed our wedding plans forever. Patience wasn't among my virtues.

But Mom hadn't given up hope for me. With words of hope and inspiration and more church-donated clothing, she helped me secure county aid until I could get going on the second job I had had in a long, long time. While looking for work, I rented a room across the street from some acquaintances I had made at our club meetings, Bob and Charlotte Jackson. I was curious about how other members stayed sober, and wanting to stay sober myself, I felt a sense of security living close to them just off Wilshire Boulevard in Hollywood. I had learned at the meetings that the purpose of the club was to help other members stay sober. In so doing, the members helped themselves, giving encouragement to those in need of it.

I landed a job in a small defense plant some distance away from my apartment, but I existed in an aura of tension, fearing and dreading the present and future. Charlotte was such a sincere member of the club that quite often she would get up and walk with me to the corner to wait until my bus came to carry me to my occupation. More than occasionally, when I called her at night, she would hurry across the street, slipping into a robe or coat as she came to wait out a period of temptation or personal remorse.

A call came one day several weeks later from one

of my girl friends who was called by most of our
mutual acquaintances, "Bromo", though her real name
was Nancy. She thoroughly believed in taking bromides for all purposes, especially for coming off a
drunk and pre-conditioning herself for one. With a
supply always in her purse, she advocated bromides
as the best nerve soother on the market. Little "Bromo"
was so small she hardly cast a shadow, but she was
almost arrogant with self-confidence, and she was
highly entertaining to all our companions from skid
row. She was a sight to behold usually; a walking
spectrum with her heavy blonde hair, blue eyes that
were encircled with various colors that accompany the
healing of a black eye. She looked like a midnight
rainbow — even I recognized her as a mixed-up alcoholic.

As she was my Southern neighbor from Texas, I
willingly caught a taxi and rushed over to her aid.
She told me over the telephone that she was going to
be thrown out of the rooming house where she lived,
but she couldn't understand why. I assured her that
I could help her with her problem. I wanted to put
the prescribed help and encouragement lessons into
practice, so I was very sympathetic anyway; and since
I had been sober for over three weeks, had a job and
was finding self-confidence, I felt sure I was the girl
for the job.

I found Bromo perched on a barstool, talking the
ears off all the barflies, as usual. She showed me that
she was drinking only beer, but only after another
beer did I manage to get her to leave with me to
return to her rooming house in hopes of reconciling
her with the landlady.

Introducing myself to the owners I found that the landlady was very perturbed and snappy as she said she had already heard all about me, and suggested that we both leave immediately. On glancing around the beautiful living room full of white leather-upholstered furniture scorched by cigarette burns to match the same on the ivory-colored end tables, I could understand Mrs. Bloomington's gruffness and position in the argument. As a result, no amount of sympathy could persuade her to let Bromo stay at least until her rent was up. I wondered how Bromo had managed such an exclusive rooming house in the first place.

Well, I had tried to practice what had been preached to me and it hadn't worked. So, I took Bromo to my little apartment after getting her a bottle to tide her over the hectic situation. She was still sleeping when I left for work at 7:00 the next morning.

When I returned from work that evening, I was stopped by the manager, who insisted that I get the girl out of my room instantly as she was drunk, destructive, unruly and making long distance calls every ten minutes. I packed her few things in preparation to leaving with her in tow, but whom should I see when the elevator descended except my railroad president, Vincent. He had been looking for me, but was presently sprawled out on a couch in the lobby, very unpresidently attired in a blue railroad shirt, on which was pinned a bright motto badge — "Pepsi Cola Hits the Spot". He was sleeping off a big one, all right.

Well, there seemed to be nothing I could do to help either of them except to join them in draining their two fifths of liquor a little later on. All the real help I had accomplished was with the old folks in the institution, so perhaps I had better let the drunks

paddle their own canoe; I drank a salute to my useless-
ness.

When I ran out of money needed even for one
more drink, I figured that now I had two sources from
which to promote my cause, so rather than call Mother
at home I decided to give her a rest and try Mom
Turpin. But for my own good, she said, she refused
to let me have money for just one drink more. I left
irritated with her and the whole world, as I continued
on my way down the street to search for my two pals
to check their prospects for getting another drink.

I didn't have many blocks to walk (but being accustomed to walking anyway, that short distance didn't
bother me) to a bar we three used to open in the
morning and leave at night, only by force. I just had
a hunch that's where they would be.

Yes, Bromo was there all right, hanging over the
bar, her tongue wagging from her loaded gills. When
she saw me, she mourned that Vincent had been arrested for picking up a radio "by mistake", for drinking money. Bromo started crying, asking me what to
do; I didn't know what to do with myself, let alone
her — so I cried, too. Disturbed about what to do with
the empty box Vincent left beneath her feet (the
box that had once contained the portable radio) we
stupidly decided to deliver it to him in person. We
were detained at the jail — for five days.

The five days to which the judge sentenced me
could have been passed easier except for Bromo's
incessant tongue twenty-four hours a day and my
shaking nearly out of my clothes. I was in agony
with cold sweats and vomiting but my torture wasn't
enough, as the jailer marched me out of our cell (and
me thinking I'd done my five days, but actually I'd

been in only overnight). I questioned my sanity as he walked me up the tiny hallway, idly talking as we walked slowly along — to where I couldn't imagine. But I was well acquainted with this particular jailer so I wasn't afraid of where he might be leading me. Reaching the end of the hall, he looked piercingly at me and said:

"My dear, I want you to take a good look at this pitiful man, who is somebody's son."

The sight of this young man scared me to death, and I quickly turned my head and asked what was wrong — why was he showing me such a sight as sick as I was. As I stood there in awe, looking sideways at the monstrosity, the jailer continued:

"Do you know this could happen to you if you don't stop your drinking, and the very next drink could be too late. This fellow has been in a state of deetees for weeks and the medical profession of the highest order can't do a thing to help him now." I was half listening and half thinking that I was already just about in the same condition as that pitiful soul stretching his hands and feet around the wire cage to which he was confined as a wild animal.

That sight lingered long in my memory but just long enough to get out of that jail and continue my journey of drinking constantly night and day. One can't be scared into sobriety; if that were true, after that ordeal I would have had many more years of sobriety behind me.

Our other inmates didn't have much use for drunks, but one female character expressed her sympathy for me by holding a cigarette for me to puff every now and then, as I couldn't hold it. She, too, had a problem and I tried to solve the mystery of how she came

to be in jail. She explained, "I just accidentally fell
asleep in a little downtown bar where a jealous somebody had laid a half-pint bottle by my side; now I'm
having to pay the penalty due somebody else."

I was all ears and condolence as she continued,
"And to think this is the third time this has been
pulled on me, too. I'm already sorry for that judge,
because when I do get out of here, I'll see that he does
a hundred days instead of the sixty that he gave me."

Although serving five days on a drunkeness charge
wasn't a new experience for me, I felt somewhat
ashamed to return to Mom, pleading for a quarter for
just one drink to relieve my tension. Upon her re-
fusal again and her seeming lack of compassion for
me all of a sudden, I stormed out — with the laundry
man who was checking his daily route. He seemed
agreeable to giving me a ride, but it took some convincing from me before he would agree to buying me
a bottle of whiskey. For the remainder of his route,
my bottle and I were his steadfast comrades, but in
the meantime we conversed like long lost friends, as he
had been calling at Mom Turpin's for several years.
Synonymous with his trade, he was always sharp-
looking in his starched khaki uniform, over which he
wore a glistening white poplin jacket to match his
cap. He thought I was the star boarder at Mom's,
having seen me around for so long, but when late in
the afternoon I learned he was the star boarder in a
little bungalow containing two children and a wife, I
asked him to drop me off somewhere in Glendale
where I could visit some friends. I had no friends
there and never did.

My mental and physical condition reached an all
time low that evening. The hospitals and institutions

which I had previously looked upon as a refuge, suddenly provided no foreseeable hope for recovery. Clinical benefits had been in vain as I couldn't control myself after release. I was indeed a hopeless, helpless alcoholic. These were my disparaging thoughts as I occupied a lonely spot on a Glendale railroad bridge.

A gentleman whom I didn't trust as either cop or friend (whom, though, I shall forget no more than his name, and that is to my sorrow) intercepted my plans, and to him and his urgent pleas I owed my life. Contemplating whether to stop, the gentleman had crossed the bridge three times unnoticed, but when he stopped I noticed a heavy-set middle aged man in white shirt sleeves emerging from his tan automobile. He approached me as would an officer, asking my name, address, etc., yet I wanted so much to know that he wasn't another. I was in such a dilemma that the only way I could possibly face Mom Turpin again was with a drink under my belt, and as I tried talking the man into buying me a bottle, I threatened to jump off the bridge. I was already leaning forward and surely would have fallen if not jumped, but upon persuasion he provided me with a bottle of whiskey and delivered me to Mom's doorstep. He proved to be an insurance company employee who happened to recognize my fitting a description radioed in a bulletin aired over all the Los Angeles area, thanks to Mom and her club friends who had perceived through their knowledge of alcoholic habits that I might attempt such recourse.

IX

YOSEMITE HEIGHTS

As I recovered under Mom's wing again, I renewed my promise to myself that I would make a comeback and prove myself strong — to myself and all mankind; but especially to Mom. After a few days I was able to write my family that all was well, although I anticipated no answer as our correspondence had diminished again. Their replies to my letters home were returned to them stamped: "No Such Address", or "Letter Unclaimed". My futile efforts at corresponding were like those of any "wino" writing to his homefolks as he sat against a log in the woods or a cold brick wall on skid row:

"Dear Folks:
Here I am — sick, no money, no clothes and nothing to eat."

After putting down his pencil to pick up his bottle of wine; and vice versa, a meaningless postscript was added.

"P.S. If there's anything that I can do for you folks back there, just let me know."

Putting together some heretofore shadowy recollections, I verified to myself that San Francisco had a rightful place in my past records as shown in the files of the state institution, after all. I remember wandering for hours about dusk in a strange town; the wind was blowing cold from the ocean. I can't recall what clothing Mom had given me for this impromptu excursion, but I'm sure Mom, too, remembers a light-weight beige coat with a small fur collar someone at the church had donated to her for people like me. Somewhere along the way I recall stopping in a very small grocery store and having just enough nickels, I bought a box of soda crackers and a dill pickle. A little girl about twelve years old, or maybe younger considering her "Dutch Boy" haircut, came into the store to buy bubble gum. As she stared at me, I thought she was admiring my coat with the little fur collar, so I told her that it had been given to me and now she could enjoy wearing it as I didn't really need it. Slipping it on her, I noticed that it fit perfectly, as I wasn't much larger than a twelve-year-old myself. As she walked out of the store wearing the coat, I wished I knew the name of the happy little girl; none the worse for having met me.

With no coat, I couldn't hide my bottle any longer, so I was to resume my traveling with my only posses-sion in a brown grocery sack, further and further on down the tragic, sorrowful road. Several more hours passed by and it was now well into the night; I found myself at a monstrous iron gate with a latch that could be lifted easily. Closing the heavy gate behind me, I walked up to the nearest building and found the door locked.

On hearing my approach, an alert nurse opened the door and asked me in, looking to see if there was any-one else with me. She asked my name, address, etc., but I couldn't offer any information regarding my mysterious appearance at her door. I then asked her where I was and if she could help me find a doctor or a hospital, but it must have been evident to her that I was sick, in desperate need of medical aid, and also tired from walking a long way. She seemed very kind, and left to summon a doctor, but returned a few minutes later to accompany me to another part of the building.

I collapsed on a straight chair in the hall as the doctor rounded the corner of his office door. Noticing my condition and foul breath, the physician commenced a series of questions: How long had I been drinking? How had I gotten there? Why? He seemed as lost for answers as I did, I thought, as he gazed at me. He was looking at me and I was looking, too — to see just where I was. Just down the hall a few feet a tremendous room opened, and there were tiny beds lined up on both sides of the crowded ward, filled with small people who seemed young, yet old. It was a mysterious sight until the young doctor, noticing my bewilderment, said that his hospital, the place to which I had come unintentionally, was for the feeble-minded: I began to fear that he had intentions of keeping me there, even though the maze of bars was familiar equipment.

After a night's rest and an injection of paraldehyde, I was able to be a little coherent, but another injection was required before I could talk sensibly. They had asked for the name of someone to call, and frightened by being in a hospital for the feeble-minded, I tried hard to recall a definite name. I finally had to settle for the Alcoholics Anonymous Club in general, in hopes one of the members would come to my rescue. Everywhere I had ever been, the members of the society had willingly helped me, so the doctor called the club headquarters for the area. I was sorry not to be able to provide a personal reference but how could I when I wasn't able to recall my own name.

Later in the afternoon, the doctor returned to tell me that some club members were coming for me, who suspicioned that I might be the same young woman on whom they had once called long ago, judging by my description. Regardless of whether I was to be the same person they remembered, they proved loyal to their cause by coming some seventy miles from Stockton to attend me. In the meantime, I was recuperating enough to remember dear Mom Turpin's name and address. Her poor little black sheep was soon to be found again.

The A.A. members from San Francisco took me to Mom's house and there she met me, with no reproach. She definitely had the patience of Job and the sympathy of Luke as she put me to bed, where I remained for over a week; but on arising, Mom conducted me straight back to the A.A. Club meetings, where at last I was beginning to see a ray of light.

"Someday you'll make it, dear," Mom Turpin said.

A few days later, I recurred at the General Hospital, the psychiatric division where I had become quite familiar. This I intended to be my last committal. During those fourteen days, I knew I had to make an absolute and permanent recovery, or die. The latter seemed the easy way out. I had traveled a long, desolate and treacherous road down, but the road back up had made stops at Near Failure, Despondency, Doubt, and Agony. As always, it proved to be much harder doing without liquor than it was to get it under direst circumstances. It was much harder to ask God to help me than it was to make bargains with Him. I had half-prayed previously for God's help in remaining sober, then weakened. Now I had a new determination, but it was difficult to sleep at night while awaiting the arrival of dawn. Then it was time to suffer until dusk. The road uphill was full of rocks and bumps, detours and side roads.

I prayed that I would have strength and sense enough to stay for the full treatment, in the meantime to learn to understand the workings of the A.A. Club, and to accept the help from its members.

As a frequent patient at the General Hospital, I had gained much experience working with the nurses, and as I obviously enjoyed the work, one of the lady doctors to whom I was assigned often counselled me and expressed her hope that someday I'd become a nurse. In this endeavor I'd surely find complete happiness and success. She was a lovely woman in person and in character, totally dedicated to doing her best for humanity. Her words have returned to my ears many, many times since; I wish I could accomplish even a small percentage of what she has done for mankind.

I didn't feel I should return to Mom's upon my discharge, for surely I had worn my welcome completely out. But, as always, I received a most cordial greeting, with the usual fittings and fixings. With Mom's reassurance, we resumed attending the club meetings and many times she accompanied me after being nearly exhausted by her day's work. Never displaying any misgivings or suspicions, she held fast to my hand as we listened to further discussions and programs pertaining to our common goal. Though Mom may have detected some of my misapprehensions, it was evident to me that I didn't understand the doctrine or functions of the club; even after attending so many meetings and hearing so many speakers and their suggestions; even after my sincere new concentration.

There were many beautiful days that I recall during what I call "recesses" from the hospital and those days (which were pitifully few) were valuable days of sobriety that are mine never to forget, to be thankful for, every day that I live.

One of those occasions was the opportunity to go on a tour of Sutter Creek where gold was first discovered in California. A guide explained the interesting points and commented on the old monuments as we went along, and I appreciated the fact that I was sober enough to thoroughly enjoy the tour. As we left, I wondered why I couldn't stay sober and pursue all the beautiful things that were so free and interesting — just for the time it takes.

After lengthy treatments in the hospitals, I was released with another few days to face sober, which I always did. One release was the day of the Pasadena Rose Parade, and as I stood on the curb of the parade route viewing the most gorgeous sight that I had ever seen, I again realized that I had been neglecting the beautiful things of God's unrestricted world, such as the flowers that bloom fragrantly from season to season. That special parade day was a dream, and my enchanted heart yearned so badly to stay sober for the rest of my days and partake of the natural wonders; but somehow, I still had to travel further down the road of alcoholism.

I managed to have longer periods of sobriety between visits to the hospitals and to me they grew better, in that my thinking became more serious; due partially to the slight impression the A.A. Club programs were leaving at long last. From the first inkling of penetration, I noticed an interference with my drinking — I realized that I couldn't have my cake and eat it too.

These periods of recess and freedom are still vivid and dear to my heart; at least I began to realize what sobriety could mean to me. I conceived that flowers truly grew and blossomed, and that even trees bore their leaves in the Spring and shed them when Fall rolled around; and that birds had songs to thrill your ears. Now all these things are mine to enjoy, and are as free as the stars in heaven; a million wonders in a world of joy and beauty can belong to the alcoholic, too — only for the taking.

Meanwhile, I was working in another sanatorium, very similar to my previous employer's though much larger. My work was about the same in that I was still taking temperatures and blood pressures and doing general things as required in bedside care. All of these duties were taught by the registered nurse who had befriended me at the previous sanatorium. It was a wonderful experience to be back with the elderly people, taking them up in wheel chairs or supporting them as they walked, if possible. And to those confined to their beds, tempting them to eat was a challenge I usually mastered, but my attempts at conversation were more than often mastered by the fascinating tales of yore spun by the oldsters, by which I was easily spellbound.

As the sanatorium was further from Los Angeles, I found it possible only to keep in touch with Mom Turpin by telephone, though occasionally during the brief period for which there was opportunity, we attended A.A. meetings or church together. In order to be in as good a standing as possible, I dropped my family a note, though by the time they received it, they probably figured I'd likely be across the country in jail or in another hospital, considering my past and all of the surprise collect telephone calls.

After six weeks of working in the sanatorium and having a small accumulation of money, I had the temerity to try for a better paying job. With the explanation that I was to join friends in another locale, I left abruptly in the company of a supposedly married couple, the Carpenters. These people I had met on many occasions in a downtown Los Angeles bar, to which I fled as soon as my eight-hour shift was over at the sanatorium. We had had a talking marathon, discussing with great finesse, the local and national news, though I barely had time to even glimpse at the headlines on the *Los Angeles Examiner*. We had spent many hours of many weeks discussing world events before hitting upon the idea of personal introductions, but considering the lateness of the hour when this social error was discovered, I was a bit slow in determining from my past history how to introduce myself. But I was happy to meet Edwina and Calvin Carpenter, and happier to join them on an excursion trip to Yosemite Park where the pasture was surely greener, for even the cabin maids earned a nice wage. I was anxious for a change of scenery even though I knew the tourist season was nearing its end.

Even as the A.A. Club's rule-of-thumb echoed in my ears, "Don't Take that First Drink; One is too Many and a Thousand Not Enough", I found I couldn't battle that "One Day at a Time" suggestion any longer. I eagerly joined the Carpenters in a toast to our new adventure.

We were soon on our way, pulling that overloaded little house trailer hitched behind the ancient Chevrolet, slowly up the mountains, and restraining it down the other side. We traveled for two days and nights, stopping only to refuel the car with gasoline and refuel ourselves with whiskey. Yosemite was one of the few places I hadn't explored in California. As I sat in the back on and among the many blankets we were taking in case of a blizzard, I wished I was sober to enjoy more fully the beautiful sights we passed, such as El Capitan, the rock mountain reaching high in the sky, towering and magnificent even through my blurred vision. The natural splendor of Bridal Veil Falls, crystal white interspersed with everchanging colors of the rainbow was indeed a spectacle. When a little, trusting, innocent deer walked up to nibble from my hand, I felt a strange new emotion. I wondered where he went when the big bears stalked the woods at night in search for food, and as evening was coming on, a tinge of fear led me back to the awaiting car.

After getting the trailer set up, with the help of obliging campers, by late that evening I decided, following a few drinks and a good night's sleep, that I'd start on my own expedition early the next morning to see how far we'd parked from the most important spot to me — the liquor store — and how far I'd have to walk to it. I felt sure it could be bought somewhere in a place like that; I'd bought it everywhere else I'd ever been. As my companions were beer hounds, that made it a bit easier on me; I could drink my liquor and they could drink their beer. My whiskey bottle was about empty, and getting a replacement took precedence over getting a job.

Much to my dismay, I discovered that my favorite

beverage wasn't readily available in Yosemite. I had no taste for beer as it didn't quench my thirst. So with only beer obtainable, I realized I was in the wrong place again.

Where there is a will, there is a way, regardless of the direction. I had heard of a camp on the mountain so I decided to apply for a job there, in hopes that a source of liquor supply would present itself. Using my own special line at the interview — being a Southern girl, a long way from home and needing work — I found my spiel falling on the very understanding ears of a kindly gentleman; he hired me.

I found much satisfaction as I cleaned cabins and lodgers' bottles simultaneously. Hunting was better in some cabins than in others I soon discovered, and to those cabins and tenants I was particularly partial. My trailer friends didn't lack for free beer, as I figured a can or two from each refrigerator wouldn't be missed.

Inevitably, a call soon came from the manager's office and I hastened to explain that as I cleaned the quarters I always poured out all the leftover whiskey, throwing the bottles away with the trash. I didn't bother to explain my choice of adverbs — I poured that liquor down and not out. He noted that it was the first complaint of lost liquor and other alcoholic beverages in many seasons, though he and the guests usually suffered an expected loss of change, articles of apparel or personal items.

My alternate source of supply wasn't as inexpensive as that acquired from the guest cabins, but moonshine was available just down the mountain. Detection was soon to catch up with this sojourner again and the manager, the same man who hired me, also fired me;

dismissing me on the pretext that the vacation season was ending anyway. Even though he seemed concerned about my finding work to see me through the winter months, I wasn't. I hadn't been concerned about plans for the cold weather in three years, having spent that season, among many another, confined in an institution somewhere.

As I belatedly returned to the trailer home I shared with the Carpenters, I encountered an elderly man, graying attractively at fifty-five or sixty years of age. He was strolling in complete solitude, until I crossed his path. He seemed interested in me, and since he appeared to be such a nice man, I joined him on a bench, and we struck up an immense conversation. Apologizing for his appearance was a mystery to me, for his casual clothing was evidently expensive; he introduced himself as Olaf Johansen. That figures, I thought, as he was a giant of a man, fair-skinned and blue-eyed as are most Scandinavians. As he was beginning to bald, I wondered if he realized how much difference there was in our ages when he approached me, but he remained the fatherly-type.

"I've been living in Los Angeles four years since my wife died some years ago. I found myself pretty lonely in Michigan. So when the time came, I chose to retire in California and make a new set of friends."

When he said "Los Angeles", I nearly leaped with joy, but not for Olaf's reasons. He thought we surely would have some mutual friends since I, too, had come from there, but I was struck with the possibility of getting a ride back to L.A. with him. I was getting pretty sick of Edwina and Calvin — they had not even tried to get a job. I certainly hadn't let them down, as I had worked for a few weeks anyway, much to their benefit. And now that I had resorted to drinking beer, too, I could hardly wait to leave.

I asked Olaf to meet my friends at the trailer and perhaps stay for a Southern version of a favorite German dish, sauerkraut and ribs. With some emotion, I felt sorry for this lonely man and consoled him as I had those aged patients I remembered working with. I pressed my invitation and he finally accepted, first offering to buy a case of beer to complete the Southern-German menu, and he added that since he was of Swedish extraction, he rather enjoyed a cold beer occasionally.

He didn't seem too impressed with the Carpenters I could easily tell, but as we all made idle conversation with our beer, I busily tended my culinary specialty. Suddenly, a terrific explosion rocked the trailer and its occupants into a frenzy. I screamed, "It's an earthquake, and it's worse than that other one," referring to the severe tremors that July day when I was in the State Hospital, though I was careful not to mention that.

After that instant of vivid memory, I looked around at the shattered remains of a congenial evening. Pieces of things had flown in every direction, and in the midst of this almost international incident, was my new gentleman friend, covered with sauerkraut and ribs. After we had collected our scattered wits to some extent, we learned that the explosion was caused by the pressure cooker having blown to bits. I never did have a good sense of timing.

We had a slight change in menu, to peanut butter sandwiches, but when food, liquor and talk ran out, I began figuring how I could rush this big-hearted

Swede into going back to Los Angeles where supply could meet my demand. I persuaded him as we sat on the trailer steps, and had not Olaf given the Carpenters the case of beer, they would have been somewhat madder for my running out on them.

Leaving early the next morning in order to dodge some of the heavy mountain traffic, I was on the go again riding along with my handsome escort. I wondered if the trailer folks would hibernate the winter in Yosemite. For myself, I was comfortably riding toward Los Angeles to give it another whirl, enjoying the bottle of whiskey I pleaded with Olaf to buy, and an amiable conversation. We had stopped at Glacier Point, and though Yosemite had been warm and comfortable, the climate grew progressively colder as we approached the Point. While I was freezing to death in my summer slacks, Olaf insisted on taking my picture knee-deep in snow.

Although the sightseeing was delaying my return to Los Angeles, I was enjoying it immensely; there seemed to be no end to things to see in California. The highlight of my return trip was through the redwood forest, and having driven through one of the trees, I was numb with awe. I still cherish some snapshots made that day of touring, and had I not been half-sober that day, I would have doubted such marvelous creations existed.

Before we left the forest in the early afternoon, we had lunch (or rather, Olaf did; I drank mine) in a place called The Gypsy Tea Room. The tea was incidental, for they also served cocktails, so that made the day complete for me. The more I drank, the livelier I became, but the quieter Olaf became. I couldn't imagine what I had said to hurt his feelings, but I wasn't too bothered as I felt sure he would see that I got back to Los Angeles, regardless, and get me off his hands. His moodiness diminished, and we were soon resuming our hearty conversation as we sped along the highway to L.A. Laughing, Olaf said, "You know, I don't understand lots of things — but I had planned to spend the summer up in Yosemite, and here I am on my way back to L.A., just to accommodate you."

He was laughing at himself, but then, looking at me with much consternation, he asked, "Why do you drink so much? I've never seen anyone, man or woman, drink as much!"

I didn't have an answer, but before I could manufacture one, he was at his questions again. "How on earth did you get involved with that outfit, the Carpenters? You'll get in real serious trouble with strangers — especially those you latch onto in a bar. My only reason for going to Los Angeles today is to get you away from those trailer rats."

I resented his questions, remarks and advice. In my heart I knew something was wrong with the Carpenters, just like myself, and I was sorry for them and their predicament. I regretted my error in telling Olaf the truth about where I had met them, but I was to divulge further truths to him as the trip progressed. I kept drinking and he kept preaching as we drove along; he described me as a complete puzzle. He couldn't imagine himself just letting somebody lead him around, especially on such short acquaintance. I tried switching the topic of conversation from my life to his, so he woefully told me of his retirement four months ago after forty years with the same rubber company, and that he had anticipated a long, well deserved rest at Yosemite. However, his rest was short and hardly beneficial, as I had carried him on high winds during our short acquaintance.

Olaf persisted in discussing my erring ways, cautioning me what might happen if I didn't steer clear of phony people; little did he suspect he was sitting beside one.

As we neared L.A. I had convinced him that I believed every word he said; that I was wrong and always had been. Since I was to be the subject of conversation anyway, I told Olaf about my marriage to a man who lived and worked for the city we would enter a few miles ahead. At that point, I insisted we stop and see him for a few minutes. I pleaded, "I haven't seen him in four years, and I'm sure he'd be delighted to see me and meet you. I'd like him to meet you, so I could show him that I can still find friends with new cars — like yours. It's not my fault we broke up — I was worthy of much more than he gave me, so let's look him up."

We didn't have any difficulty locating Val, for after twenty-three years' service with the city, he was well known, and I hadn't forgotten my way around. Standing there in the City Hall, shaking all over, I was amazed to note that he didn't mince words in public as he answered Olaf's suggestion that we, as "ex's" might like to be alone for a few minutes.

"You two might even patch things up after all these years," connived the older, more romantic man. But I wondered if he were desperately trying to get rid of me!

"There's not enough patches in Los Angeles County to patch up that marriage," Val retorted. "She's just the biggest booze hound I've ever known or seen, and always will be, from the looks of her. If she hasn't already drained you of everything you possess, she will. If you're smart, you'll take my advice and shake her. If you're short of cash already, I'll pay her fare back to the South just to keep her off my back for a while. She blows in every two or three years — much too often."

Olaf was confounded by Val's revelation, and I was somewhat perplexed that Val hadn't let bygones be bygones. (Injecting a note out of chronological order, I'm sure he's been happier missing my impromptu visits now for over thirteen years.)

As Olaf had been warned, he was to be dragged down by my incessant needs. He abandoned me as a hopeless burden, though he tried to help me as many people before him and after had done. Still allowing alcohol to continue tearing my life into shreds, and submitting to its complete control, I had fallen to still another low ebb. With my very soul in agony I again resorted to suicidal plans. Suicide was beginning to have a sweeter appeal; in fact it seemed the only course. I couldn't go on living on alcohol, and it was impossible to survive without it. With mutual disgust between all those hospitals and jails and me, there was no haven to be sought; not even as a coward.

X

HOME AGAIN, HOME AGAIN

As a homing pigeon, I alit at Mom's doorstep again late in 1948, in the familiar depraved condition. Feeling too miserable to appreciate her usual welcome, Mom Turpin nonetheless opened her door and took me in. My lack of stamina showed pitifully as she tried repeatedly and laboriously to help me conquer my weakness. Often we would find ourselves reviewing the past and contemplating the future at 2 a.m. in the morning. As usual, I promised to play my role straight.

Gaining sobriety for just a day or two seemed an impossibility, but I had done it before with less strain. During those brief interludes, I fully realized that I had to help myself; to meet God halfway. I must stop compromising with Him. I remembered during the current abstinence that one of the steps toward recovery was to refuse yourself the first drink, as it was the one causing the damage. I didn't understand this difficult rule, as my hand seemed magnetized toward the first and many subsequent drinks.

Weeks passed on, and again Mom Turpin called my family, telling them that I was with her again and not to worry; that she knew someday I'd get over "alcoholism". She kept me busy, for on weekdays we attended A.A. Club meetings together. I ran errands to and from her church while Mom made visits to the tuberculosis sanatorium some distance away, taking cook-

ies and little gadgets to those truly physically sick
people. On Sundays we went to church every time
the door opened, and I often thought it miraculous
that God had sent me to Mom, a dedicated member
of the Christian Church, in which I had been reared.
If we sat at night to have our earnest discussions, Mom
always had handiwork in her lap, and a smile on her
face.

Trying to taper off with a daily half-pint of whiskey,
my half-sober thoughts wandered back to my institution days, sober and happy ones for the most part,
the part when I helped care for those elderly persons.
I had a remote dream, but on many occasions as Mom
Turpin recalls, I began making plans to have a nursing
home of my own. With more imagination, I suggested
to Mom that she fly to see me and my nursing home.
She laughingly told me, "I know that you can do just
that, if you want to; but I'm not so sure about my
flying."

With Mom providing the essentials again, I found
work in the sanatorium where I had been employed
before my Yosemite expedition. Once again the same
sweet nurses greeted me, still willing to accept me,
help and encourage me as I went about my daily
chores in sickness and confusion. Regaining some lost
weight and forcing myself to rest in hope of eventually
sleeping, I limited myself to that half-pint when again
there was no will left. The self-imposed restriction
proved hard to maintain, and I was soon making daily
trips to the liquor stores, at the same time going to
the weekly A.A. Club meetings. I was ashamed of
myself, for with the security of a job and regular pay-
days I had the opportunity to provide myself with a

good future, instead of scurrying to and fro like a dumb animal.

An added problem of homesickness presented itself to a scene already complicated with guilt and incompetence, but I was anxious to see my family again now that I could afford the cost of the trip. If they knew I was drinking only every other day, they would welcome me after several years absence, perhaps. Shirley, whom I had not seen in nearly nine years was returning to the States and home, and this information highlighted Mom's most recent call in my behalf. So I gave a thirty-day notice to my employer, and set about making plans for my much desired reunion, which I hoped would be for three weeks.

Once again I proudly got across the State of Texas without interruption, and meeting my family at the bus station was a real surprise for us all, myself included, for I was quite sober. The family had changed somewhat during my four-year absence, but the greatest change was the addition of someone to the family circle. Standing in the pouring rain to meet her aunt was a little red-haired girl in a little plaid raincoat with matching hat and umbrella with raindrops dripping from the curls her rotating parasol hadn't protected. Polly, who had been married four years, had been blessed with this darling little daughter whom I nicknamed "Tink" at first sight. I feared that even the baby had heard all about me and I pledged to make amends to my family on this visit. And as a child could, Tink became the dearest little girl to enter my life. I'm so thankful that she was too young to know just what to expect when she saw her bus-riding aunt for the first time. My many prayers for her happiness and well-being have been answered, for she

is an "A" student in one of the South's most outstanding colleges. However, there was little twelve-
year-old "Beaver" who did remember my episodes and
failures. My prayer is that he has forgiven me now
that he is a grown young man — the image of his
father, Red.

Mother, still the most courageous of mothers, and
understandably a bit grayer, rejoiced in having her
children about her, reveling with satisfaction in her
adorable grandchildren. Red, despite his heart ail-
ment, came home for the reunion. I was amazed at
the mass of adults about me, but at Buck in particular;
no longer a kid brother, but a near-graduate from law
school.

Inquiring as to the whereabouts of Shirley, whom
I was particularly eager to see, they told me that she
was working some four hundred miles away but that
she would arrive the next day to complete the reunion.
I hoped I would be sober when she arrived, for I had
become sentimental and depressed as we alcoholics
so often do, as my thoughts wandered way back to
when Polly and Buck were such little ones. Tink
reminded me of Polly waiting for me to come home
from work, when we were all so young and innocent.
I tried dismissing those memories as getting too sentimental might lead me to that Air Port Liquor Store to
do some checking. Shirley arrived at a good time,
and nine years had been mighty good to her.

I had looked forward to the sight of her, but with
apprehension. I hadn't heard from her in all those
years and dreaded that perhaps she would reject me
for what the family surely must have reported to her.
A mountainous resentment formed within me, ashamed
for myself and disappointed for fear the family might

have revealed my weakness in their letters overseas to her. I hoped with all my heart that she didn't suspect the awful truth about my past. I was in much sympathy for myself and my iniquities; yet pitiless toward my family for possibly having divulged them.

I became ashamed that I had allowed my imagination to contribute additionally to the family's emotional strain, for several years ensued before Shirley learned of my committals and repeated failures, and only then by being the first to read the story of my struggle and strife.

I asked her one day soon after the reunion why she had never written to me and she said, "Sister, nobody ever knew your right and legal name or address when I asked, so let me make a note of it right now, so we can correspond as sisters should!" ·

I had always petitioned the court to return my maiden name following the divorces and I luckily could give her the same name she knew so well, thus avoiding any and all explanations for the time being.

With family ties secured, I was happy to accept her invitation to return to her new home with her, understanding her job responsibility and limited time. Once there and settled in her apartment, I began wondering if she should be told of her "Big Sister's" having been termed a hopeless alcoholic, and decided it would be better to inform her myself in my own way than for her to learn an exaggerated version, if there could be one. On our arrival in the city where Shirley was employed at an Air Base, I immediately called Alcoholics Anonymous to inquire about their meeting place, time, etc. Then I invited Shirley to attend a meeting with me at the local chapter of a club to which I belonged; and not suspecting even slightly that it would be Alcoholics Anonymous, she agreed to accompany me (not that she would have refused otherwise).

Shirley was somewhat amazed and very interested in the mechanics of the club, so together, we enjoyed the congeniality with which we, as visitors were included. She hadn't grasped much of the ultimate purposes of the club from my interpretation — after all, I wasn't an avid, true follower myself as yet. At last she knew of my weakness and disease, but I didn't wholly convince her that I wasn't attending the meetings for the purpose of hunting a husband, either. I was tempted to relate my entire marital history, but after a second thought, I decided perhaps she couldn't tolerate the shock.

Among the acquaintances we made at the meeting was a sharply dressed gentleman whom I figured was sporting a new outfit to celebrate his vowed sobriety. Alcoholics don't usually care about appearances while under the influence, I noted, but at other times, can be quite presentable and proud. Anyway, his bright, amber, suede sport coat was eye-catching, complemented by his beige trousers, and enhanced by his gray-tinged hair. Introductions soon followed and I later learned that all my calculations were correct.

Ford carried a gift of gab that entertained us over coffee and French fries, telling us fabulous stories about himself, his experiences as a construction worker, his length of sobriety, etc., and judging from the tip he left the waitress in the cafe to which he had invited us, I decided he carried money to burn. He courteously escorted us back home and he seemed especially interested in me as he said good night, first suggesting that he take me out the following week to see the historic sights of the city. Being a stranger in a strange city again, I accepted.

The landlady was openly suspicious of my sister and me as the former occupants drank heavily and entertained men. In her caution, she could have overlooked me as far as courting was concerned, for I had no plans for male companionship, much less Shirley's suspicion of my searching for a mate through A.A.! Her suspicions regarding my drinking were wellfounded, though upon noticing the landlady's glass of beer on the table, I knew we'd get along all right. We grew to know and love our landlady, and little did we know that we would meet again someday in the fulfillment of my dream. Pretending to be more stern than her usual nature, she reminded us of her position, being young and alone, thus demanding that we be ideal tenants, even as she accompanied us upstairs to Shirley's lovely apartment. I thought Shirley extremely lucky to have such a swank place, complete with a canopy bed.

Shirley was admittedly a light, social drinker who could take it or leave it, but unaware that I was such an acute alcoholic, she brought a bottle of whiskey home one night to fix herself a drink before dinner. Soon after dinner it was half-empty, as I had poured the top half into another bottle and carefully tucked it under the sofa cushions for my morning enjoyment.

We received a letter from Mother a few days later announcing her plans to pay us her first visit. We happily anticipated her arrival, and I issued Ford, my new gentleman friend, an invitation to go with Shirley and me to meet her at the train. A few days later when Mother arrived, a snappy little sailor-boy graciously helped her step down, and Ford courteously took her arm as we escorted her to his borrowed car. She greeted Shirley first, and turning her attention then to me, I could detect from her expression that she thought I had lost no time in finding a new boyfriend.

The next item on our agenda for the day was preparing a steak dinner together at our apartment, to which we also invited Ford. Conversation was stifled somewhat by Mother's peculiar mood, so soon after dessert I bade Ford good night, considering perhaps that Mother was tired from her trip. Mother and Shirley promptly retired for the night, and I soon followed by passing out from so many snitched drinks. During the course of the evening, I had made many a trip to the bathroom, steadily sipping on Shirley's remaining half.

As soon as Shirley left for work the next morning, I left also to purchase myself another bottle of whiskey, leaving Mother still sleeping. Upon my return from the store, Mother went into a tirade over the previous night's incident, yet she blamed no one for my getting drunk when I sought excuses. I further dismissed Mother's reproach when later in the day I uncovered the bottle I'd hidden in the sofa. I drank to such unusual excess for one day that an agonizing case of delirium tremens attacked as I lay on the sofa.

After Shirley called acquaintances from the A.A. Club to come over for assistance, it was decided to send me to the hospital. I remembered nothing of their coming, or of being in transit to the emergency room. My faculties were failing again, but on reviving a few days later, I was dismissed.

Meanwhile, our mother continued her visit, though not under ideal circumstances. She distrusted everyone and especially feared my arrival from the sanatorium near our apartment, where I had found a job. The doors to the apartment were locked after each entry or departure, and it was a burden for my sister to arrange a check on Mother during the day. Occasionally the landlady came upstairs to visit with Mother, only to have the door relocked immediately. Her emotional state was a mystery to all of us, and as I had taken the job near our apartment especially to be near her during her three week visit, I was particularly puzzled. As she boarded the train back to her home, I made a solemn vow that I would quit drinking and live up to her expectations, as I knew my actions contributed to her qualms.

Ford called on me often and it was a surprise to me that I found myself liking him and enjoying his company. He seemed very stable and particularly concerned about my drinking problem, which I appreciated inasmuch as he had evidently much stamina toward conquering his own problem. Several times Ford borrowed a car and on one occasion as we passed a huge cemetery, he laughingly said that once he had greatly improved its appearance. He had been assigned the job of cutting all that grass, doing two days for one, working out a jail sentence for drunkenness. I thought him lucky, in a way, as I had never received any two-for-one deal, and I'd been in lots of jails. Knowing him as well as I did at the time, I couldn't imagine him in such a predicament, but as I've said elsewhere, alcohol has no favorites.

It came as a complete surprise and delight when he proposed to me one night during our regular date. We still occasionally jokingly argue as to who asked whom, but this proposal was thankfully different from the ones in California that I embarrassingly remembered not only accepting, but sometimes initiating.

We were married a few months later, and as his vocation required it, we moved often from town to town. Although I had been considered "transient" nearly all of my adult life, I began to tire of the constant moves. Eventually we settled on a more permanent basis, though only for a short while. We rented an apartment, and there were times when we hung on a pretty low limb, confronted by our mutual problem as well as the usual marital variety. We attended the A.A. Club meetings occasionally, but more than just occasionally, I resumed my old drinking habits despite all I, my husband, or anyone could do to dissuade me.

It was back to the hospital routine again to which I was so accustomed; glucose feedings and assorted injections to revive me. With no particular facilities in that locale for alcoholics, I went to the psychopathic division with its barred windows and locked doors; I was accustomed to that, too. Many days of confinement were spent only to be repeated again and again. Ford stayed right with me, very attentive and sympathetic, visiting me daily. But there was the consequential rejection by friends and family. Shirley wanted no part of me — no longer visited or called me; and I couldn't succeed in reaching her by telephone to hear her voice. Resentment and distrust twisted my mind to the breaking point, and my condition was nearing the final climax for my devoted husband, too. Even in my utmost despair, I knew he was on my side, but I wondered why God had forsaken me, letting my prayers go unanswered.

With revenge the basic reason, I thought of one

scheme with which to retaliate Shirley's rejection; move away from her. Ford, after much persuasion, agreed to leave for California so I could forget Shirley, the rest of my family, the sacrifice and heartache I had brought upon us all. I wanted desperately to regain their love and respect, but not having it for myself, I found solace in retreating with more alcohol.

During the next two years in California, I lived in utter torment, attempting to stay sober for many, varying intervals. It was always difficult and I often prayed for strength to resist the temptation even as I pushed open the door into a liquor store. Even after a month of hard earned sobriety, I blamed God for failing me as I weakened at last to surrender again. I felt that God wasn't doing His part — yet feigned that I was surely doing mine to the utmost.

Occasionally I allowed God a little more of my own patience in rectifying His failure to save me from myself. With more reverence, I pleaded forgiveness and prayed for strength more fervently, and compared my heavy cross with that of our Saviour's. I tried so hard to follow the narrow white line, yet to my own consternation, I failed more often than not. I hoped for a miracle overnight — a painless, simple solution to the problem. For my own lack of perseverance toward that ultimate goal, I contradicted myself as I begged forgiveness. I could not accept my full share of responsibility; I pleaded for more strength from Above. Repeatedly I slipped, following those spasmodic efforts, into the pit again.

Meanwhile, I was re-accepted at the sanatorium from which I had months previously requested the leave of absence to attend the family reunion. I was fortunate to have been reinstated in good graces, though the good graces were short-lived. The manager of the infirmary sympathized with me as I remained my own worst enemy, but even she possessed limited endurance.

It was a pleasure to introduce Ford to Mom Turpin, and we visited back and forth as often as we could, but due to my night hours at the sanatorium and Ford's long daytime hours, much of our visiting was done by frequent telephone calls. However, she was delighted that I was so happily married.

On hearing that I continued to be a problem alcoholic, an institution doctor who had befriended me, called and offered to pay my transportation costs back to the South in hopes that home would aid in combatting my disease. Talking as we often did over the telephone, he hadn't known of my trip home and subsequent return to California, happily married; but he knew of the endless and repeated confinements chalked to my score in the more recent months. It was a pleasure to resume our telephone visits like old times. He was happy that I had married and pleased that we were coming to the hospital to visit him on a Tuesday.

Something minor arose that prevented our keeping the Tuesday date, but Ford and I arrived instead on the following Thursday. After looking for him all over the familiar grounds and having the nurses call first his office and then page the entire hospital, we still couldn't locate him. When the nurses told me of his delight that I was coming for a sober visit, I became more eager to see my old friend; so we hurried across the grounds to his home in hopes of visiting a short while before he retired for the evening. Getting no response after knocking on both doors and calling to him, we decided he simply couldn't be located and returned to our home in Glendale.

What a grievous shock came early the next morning when from the hospital came news that my favorite doctor had been found dead in his home later that night; death resulting from heart failure. By not opening his unlocked door, I was spared the sight of his lifeless form, but I regretted that I hadn't seen him again before God called him away.

I hope he knows my life was restored in proper order, due in a large part to his kindness and understanding as he worked relentlessly with my sunken soul as well as my ailing condition, even after I had been formally discharged from his direct care in the hospital. He must have innumerable stars in his crown, and I hope one of them is in my name. He truly lived and practiced his faith, and imparted much to me as he explained his religious beliefs. He knew I had lost both faith in God and confidence in myself, and often told me of his prayers in my behalf. Among my treasured possessions are his letters of encouragement, urging me to join him in prayer, stressing the importance of true faith in recovery. His patient understanding and therapy in well chosen words were as beneficial as the medication he prescribed.

XI

FINDING MYSELF

Remaining in California offered little consolation — evidently Shirley and the rest of the family weren't suffering as a result of my absence. Ford, quite naturally, wasn't entirely happy there, so we decided to return to the South. As Ford had been active during the construction boom, making an excellent salary and with what I had left from my own salary after paying my essential bills, we had accumulated enough to buy ourselves a new automobile. We drove cross-country seeing new sights, and some "old" ones from my new perspective in an automobile rather than from Greyhound bus windows. Our leisurely trip through the Painted Desert was memorable. Soon, we were eastward enough to visit with family and old friends enroute to resettling nearer our homes.

We rested from the long journey for a few days in our small apartment, and in the meantime a construction job materialized for Ford. It required that we part temporarily, but as it paid well, there was some compensation for his going to New York. Having decided not to accompany Ford, I investigated a nearby sanatorium that operated especially for alcoholics. Upon my inquiry for a job, I was hired for general duty there. One particular patient, a banker from the Carolinas, is outstanding in my memory. I figured he must be a regular guest, as he seemed well acquainted with the nurses and staff doctors. While tidying his

room and making his bed one morning, I confirmed
my suspicions, though I didn't understand the situation, when a "jigger" of whiskey was brought to him
on schedule.

He didn't suspect that I, too, was an alcoholic as I
began a casual conversation, into which I planned to
pack a punch line. I subtly questioned him as to his
definition and description of an alcoholic, and about
his own personal drinking. Slowly I led up to the
point of telling him that I had heard of a club called
Alcoholics Anonymous, and recommended it to him.
My solicitation failing again, he interrupted me at the
very mention of A.A., and said dejectedly:

"They can't help me now, I'm afraid." Downing his
jigger of whiskey, he confided further, "I've been told
since being here, that I signed my own resignation as
Vice-President of my hometown bank after twenty-
six years — I've ripped it; nothing will help me now."

My pace slackened in order that I might hear the
rest of his story. Morosely, the shrinking form of a
man continued, "I may as well invest in this hospital
and just take my bed and board here for the rest of
my life. I've never done a thing like that before, but
since I can't control the future, I may as well stay
here. Besides, my wife has started divorce proceedings now."

As I listened, I watched his hands and body tremble,
saturated in a cold sweat. How sorry I felt for that
sick soul as I recalled my own wretched experiences
in a slow hell. In him I noted the progressiveness of
the disease, no respecter of persons.

The hope that I could be of some help to others thus
afflicted proved unlikely as a result of my own lack of
fortitude and perseverance. The inevitable loss of my

job coincided with Ford's return from New York, where he had gotten pneumonia.

While Florida-bound to seek greener pastures, I enjoyed the coastal scenery in all its glory with sea gulls swooping about over the silvery sands and rippling, white-capped waves. I recalled our wedding day as we sped along toward the very town in which we were married, thinking it quite coincidental that Ford's work should return us there.

I was greatly relieved that Shirley had been transferred to Tennessee. This eliminated her chance to openly and deliberately avoid seeing me, as our new home was not too distant from Shirley's former base. I still resented heavily her total and continued rejection of me. That ill emotion, burdened with disease, dragged me further down. Additional hospital treatment was the traditional result. Recovery was hampered by those prevailing, warped emotions with which I usually suffered; jealousy, revenge, rebelliousness and self-pity. Then on discharge from the hospital, I was to return to a small, dismal and lonely apartment, from which Ford was called to long hours on his job. To cure my loneliness, it was all too easy to get a bottle of whiskey; the very first drink of which took me straight back through the emergency entrance of the hospital, to relive the usual agony and endure the usual treatment prerequisite to another release. Such is the vicious circle of an alcoholic.

My personal recession met with an economic one, prompting a move into another Southern state where Ford had opportunity to work with another construction company. The town was very small, affording very little entertainment but requiring much imagination on my part to keep busy and interested in doing something — anything. To be physically active and constructively engaged was a method of progress toward the sobriety grade; I remembered that from my club programs, though heretofore I had seemed to lack initiative. Having little choice of the few resources available to meet my needs, I found some interest in taking part in the activities of a small church, though it wasn't of my former denomination.

Every Wednesday afternoon I met with a group of little girls from seven to twelve years of age, who probably taught me more than they themselves learned from our chosen project. I had never enjoyed many of the domestic arts, and certainly knew nothing of sewing, but I vowed that somehow the girls and I would dress fifteen dolls to send overseas to other little girls who otherwise would have had little or no Christmas. While shopping for the dolls, materials, scissors, needles, thread, etc., I realized that making these gifts for the happiness of others was going to be fun. I felt a radiance and satisfaction that is still appreciated for all its worth. All too soon our project was completed, and I was extremely proud of my class (and myself, too, secretly) as the attractively dressed dolls were held by the minister for the congregation to see.

Having been a near saint for a change, I soon found myself on the other side of the gate. Perhaps I didn't realize that everyone has a cycle in their everyday experiences of life, varying in degrees and extremes and at fluctuating intervals. What seems such a simple summation today was then a selfish problem, and I continued drinking.

We thought it would be convenient and somewhat of an economy measure for me to stay with Ford's family while he took a short assignment in a nearby town. We were not well-acquainted, so I didn't look forward to an extended visit in close quarters. I arrived in a nervous, irritable state, and truly wanting to resist a drink, I made an appointment with a doctor who consented to a prescription of nerve pills, which in alcoholic language are also known as "goof balls". The drug took its intended effect, and I soon relaxed to the point of no resistance against that first drink. As predicted and preached at the club meetings, I couldn't resist another, then another, until too late. Then, though I don't recall it, the doctor was summoned.

After a few days of hospitalization, my husband came for me, but I had in the meantime decided that I should find new territory, leaving Ford to do as he pleased, and allowing myself to do the same. On returning to his folks' home for a brief apology for my actions I accepted his offer to take me to that familiar scene of departures, the bus depot. Supplied with a ticket, I headed for a place, any place, but my ticket was good for only one hundred and fifty miles.

With such a vaguely planned destination, I decided to make a stopover and call on some friends I hadn't seen in fifteen years. From the phone booth at the bus station I announced my pending visit, and then proceeded to spend my only six dollars on a fifth of whiskey with which to greet them, as they were nice enough to come for me.

We brought one another up to date with family news and past events, but I elaborated somewhat as it came my turn. I described vividly the places I had been (with many exceptions and many more insertions). The little daughter of the family looked up at me in amazement as I rambled on and on with stories from a glorious past. When I took a split second for another breath in which to describe further the fabulous events of my life, she found time enough in which to get her few words in edge-wise. The eight-year-old realist exploded my fascinating oral dreams as she announced, "I don't believe you, Auntie."

Well, I had to get away from there, or finally admit deception. Even a child could see through me. I generously gave my friends all my possessions, bag and baggage, and a fond adieu.

Dazedly intending to go into town some six miles away, I was intercepted enroute by the highway patrol who promptly noticed my need for a jail cell. The officers on duty and the other prisoners were quite cordial and understanding, which was a rarity, but I found another astounding feature of this confinement — the bars and floors had already been cleaned. The officers thought me sober enough for release after a few days, but I knew I was a weak, shaking, sick, vomiting and probably a dying alcoholic. In desperate need of treatment or just a friend or familiar face in this strange, teeming city, I found my way to the Welfare Department for aid.

On confronting a sympathetic and lovely lady sitting at her desk, unable to speak audibly myself, she spoke first. "Here is a dollar — go out and get a bite to eat while I try to locate some of your people. Come back in an hour when you're feeling better, and by then someone surely will have come to help you." As she had been unable to derive much useful information from me, she scanned my purse and billfold for leads and clues as I gaped helplessly.

I didn't happen to be hungry at the moment, but as a wild, starving animal seeking prey, I sought a liquor store or bar. I finally walked into a tiny cubicle and almost immediately a man asked if he could treat me to a drink. Immediately, I accepted his generosity, and suggested that we order the biggest one available. Not due to the size or weight of the drink or glass, he actually held the glass to my mouth. When I finally got it all down, my trembling subsided, but the pangs in my stomach were like ferocious ocean waves.

Still holding fast to the dollar designated for a meal, I made my way back to the welfare office, not expecting to find friend, family or even foe awaiting. Uppermost in my clouded mind was the thought of redeeming a small bracelet that I had obligingly left as collateral for the dollar.

When I finally found the lady's office, she said, "I've contacted your family and I'm sorry to say that they told me not to send you to them. They said they couldn't help you, anyway; so you can't go there. But I'm still trying to locate your husband."

Looking up through the haze, a familiar face approached, and as he neared I almost cried, saying, "Here he comes now. He's come back to help me."

My husband thanked her graciously for the time she had taken with me, and asked if anything was owed. We refunded the same dollar bill and I offered her the bracelet as a token of my own appreciation. Then a firm arm around my back led me to the car. I thanked God that Ford had come.

As he searched along the busy highway for a motel vacancy, Ford understandingly withheld any criticism or upbraiding. He sensed that I was suffering in agony as never before; and I sensed that I couldn't go further down — I had to start going up; realizing as I rode beside him how critically ill I had become. New fervor entered my prayers as I pleaded with God to give me another chance. I wouldn't need another.

I suddenly knew God was with me, aware at last that He always had been; I knew it was God's plan for me to suffer at death's door. I was grateful for His patient interventions as I ruined the life He had given me. I was ready to make amends and regain a self-respecting place in the world, among a loving family and amid a host of friends. I was also very nearly dead.

The "Vacancy" sign finally appeared, and after getting my thin unconscious form onto the bed, Ford left momentarily to inquire at the cafe beside our motel as to where he could locate a doctor. From the description given of my condition, the doctor arrived within a few minutes after my husband's call, and they rushed me to the small, local hospital where glucose, paraldehyde — the works — were administered in haste but with efficiency.

As I rallied I sensed the activity about me, but I couldn't reason or remember anything prior to entering the motel drive; except that I had fallen to the bottom of a depthless well. When I had responded sufficiently, the doctor spent much time each day discussing the crisis through which I had miraculously lived. He was an effective doctor, but I attributed my survival to God's answering my urgent and sincere pleas. The physician warned me of the dangers of future alcoholic seizures, the very next of which I couldn't hope to outlive, and recommended contacting a group of people in his town who had proven a good record for themselves in reclaiming otherwise lost lives. I told him I was familiar with the club to which he referred, and now that I had renewed faith in God, my confidence would be restored to cooperate with the Alcoholics Anonymous program, gladly and fully.

I had hardly spoken the thought and promise when several members from the local A.A. group came into my room, bringing flowers and compassion. I had only by the Grace of God pulled through those past several days, and to be remembered by man as well was a bonus I didn't expect. Their efforts were typical of all club members, whom I can repay only by staying sober — which is all any of us want in recompense. I fully decided that the club and its members was a worthy, wonderful organization of which I could be a useful member. In spite of my old suspicions and doubts of the club, I now recognized its well-founded principles and steps, and was anxious to follow those proven methods.

The doctor released me into the warm, loving care of my husband. I was grateful that God had blessed me with him, and I asked a silent prayer that Ford would forgive me and continue his untiring moral support that I was surely to need. With God on my side, I would not fail again. To me He had performed another miracle, and it occurred to me how often we mortals overlook or forget the wonderful things His Hand hast Wrought. He had watched over me, and I felt confident that He would help me find my peace. With God, all things are possible.

As I filled my heart and mind with positive thoughts and emptied them of the old and ugly ones, I aspired to remodel myself. Bit by bit, little by little, I discharged that accumulation of ill will and emotional distress that had plagued my life, as well as the lives of many of my family and friends. Where once I had hated, I concentrated love; and I exerted all the patience I could muster where once I had none. In offering help and understanding to others, I found a great reward for myself.

I know now that every human has weaknesses; I know that I'm not the only soul in the world to suffer disappointment or remorse as does naturally occur along life's course. I learned to accept things for what they are; and myself for all my defects. I learned to live each day for and unto itself, and in doing so I happily realized that many months had passed since my last tantalizing taste of alcohol. But before I could do any of this, I had to be honest in all things — with myself in particular. The word honesty is as important in my daily life today as my bottle ever was during my darker years.

Knowing that "idleness is the devil's playhouse", I forced on myself a rigid schedule both at home and at work, which I found in a nursing home especially for aged patients. Though I forbade myself to review all my lost years, I had at the most, gained experience in the field of nursing and I occasionally allowed my memory to return to the scene of those elderly, degenerated souls with whom I had worked and cared for in so many institutions. Memory of them in their efficient surroundings returned the minute I entered the building in which my newest employer housed her aged guests. Conditions were in a shameful state, and I wished for a magic wand with which to change it all. The least I could do was to try to make my new charges a little happier in their dismal environment. I became joyously engrossed in every detail of the home and labored willingly.

The owner of the rest home wherein at last I was finding both usefulness and happiness, a lady, evi-

dently noticed my enthusiasm. Though she was every
bit as unpredictable and impulsive as I had ever been,
she surprised me one day by asking me to buy her
interest. I wished very much that I could, but our
finances wouldn't allow even the thought; though
through the years of worse difficulty I had often
dreamed of operating my own nursing home someday,
discussing my hopes and dreams with Mom Turpin,
often in the middle of the night. That little seed of
ambition began to sprout after so many years, the first
indication arising when I asked one of my favorite
little lady patients if she'd like to go home with me
for a short visit. She was a widow, having lost her
doctor-husband many years ago, and was now recuperating from having broken both legs while visiting in
her sister's home. Understanding that she had not
been happy, I felt genuinely sorry for her. The more
we each thought of the possibility, the more we leaned
toward more permanent arrangements in my care of
her. My old dream was crying to materialize, but I
explained to her that our apartment was very small
and that we wouldn't be able to afford a larger place.
Regardless, I could hardly wait to get home and discuss
the proposition with Ford.

Together we weighed the practical aspects against
my intense desire to start my own nursing home, and
the decision came in my favor. By borrowing $700
from Ford's sister and renting a larger house, we
proceeded on a very meager scale. Besides the
necessity of a hospital bed, we needed to add somewhat to our household necessities, which consisted
of, as an example, two plates, two cups, two saucers,
two each of the silverware, one lone pot, and a can
opener. We were willing to struggle along, realizing

that we had to crawl before we walked, but aspiring to much greater and better things. Considering the shape of our credit rating and past history, our aspirations were mighty; but we both had acquired a will to succeed.

Following a brief appointment at the hospital to have the casts removed from her legs, the ambulance brought my first guest, and she has remained with me since, dear to my heart. Attending her and accomplishing all the household chores involved a lot of hard work and perseverance. However, having found that trait within myself, I found it possible to maintain a pitiful linen supply, washing and ironing all the bedding as it was changed.

The newer house was tremendous in size, and we welcomed the arrival of our second guest, who also transferred to my care. With the reality of a complete nursing home unfolding, I gladly accepted the additional responsibility. Two more of all the essentials were required, but were secured readily by the new patient's board paid in advance.

I worked night and day. After getting my first patient in her walker, and the other prepared for the day, the cleaning, cooking and re-cleaning began. I had not a spare moment; for this I was delighted. Ford helped in a most valuable way, even though he had already devoted a full day to his trade. We happily tended to many things together, and enjoyed a mutual satisfaction in realizing that we were well on the way to fulfilling an old dream.

Before many months passed, we were caring for five guests, and with a little selfishness I felt that they truly belonged to me. Every plan was made for and scheduled around them, and therein I found happiness growing and glowing. I found much enjoyment in loading four of them in our automobile for an afternoon ride. Frequently, Ford would treat us all to dinner across the beautiful bay on Sundays, careful to return home in time for their families' usual Sunday visits. Even though my cup was filled to overflowing, we were at last showing enough profit to hire a cook, and as adept as she was we were all willing to relinquish the Sunday excursions across the bay for dinner at home. I was proud of our progress and happy to be needed.

After nearly a year, I started making plans for a larger house. Fearing that we could never even hope to borrow the amount of money required, I nevertheless enjoyed drawing and redrawing plans for a new house. Often I would sit in the den and sketch for hours after I had made the final check into the rooms of my "family" for the night. The sketches were not elaborate (most of the time I was quite practical) but I had little hope of raising capital for even the simplest plan. At the height of my enthusiasm one day, I called the City Welfare Department for additional information on which to build my dream, and was referred to the State for pertinent rules and regulations. In response to my inquiry, the State inspector visited me to learn the details of my plans — how many patients were to be accommodated, how financing was to be arranged, and the building site. He informed me that the City had to approve everything before the State could move on any decision.

City regulations required that fifty feet be allowed on each side of the proposed building, and the department gladly offered to be of further assistance if needed. My pipe-dreaming had netted a lot of information, but without a dollar, my plans, hopes and I were stalemated.

However, one night soon after gathering all the foregoing information, my first patient offered to let us borrow $1500 with the usual rate of interest, which would be an investment for her; so I resumed my planning. With every real estate agent in town, I began my search for larger quarters in an existing building, and I nervously toyed with the hopes of not renewing our present lease, which was soon to expire. We continued to look for over a year, and at times I was so disheartened that I regretted to suspect that perhaps I wasn't worthy or capable of running a large nursing home anyway.

September brought about the decision to renew the lease on the present property, as we hadn't succeeded in finding adequate or acceptable housing that was available for $1,500 initial cost. With so much at stake, frustration added to my disappointment. But I had learned to accept and live with disappointments and declared that I could make do where we were, giving thanks for our marvelous progress.

Two weeks passed, and still fighting a case of disillusionment, I stretched out across the couch to scan the day's paper. As a newly entered advertisement of property for sale caught my eye, I realized its possibilities and promptly called the real estate agent again. The cook Melina shared in my excitement, but as she had become somewhat pessimistic, she advised, as she stood in the kitchen doorway with her hands rammed deep in the pockets of her blue-checked apron, "You just forget that house right now before you burden yourself with more disappointment. We're bound to be here another year, and we'll make this old house do fine."

But I had already started getting dressed and ready to accompany the real estate agent out to see the house described as being ideally suited to my new set of plans which had withered to a wing addition to our present house.

I felt an exhilarant presence of God as we approached the gate to four acres of beautifully landscaped grounds near the edge of town, and there in the midst of a lovely lawn stood a charming, comfortable-looking house in excellent condition. My heart fluttered as we looked inside the house to find, as the agent had noted, one of the State's main requirements; it was equipped with a brand-new forced-air heating system. Another requirement was met, I soon learned, by the installed floodlighting system on the exterior of the house.

As we strolled over the grounds, it seemed to me that the bright flowers, singing birds, and the lovely hand-laid rock rimmed fish pond, centered with a minature light house, were omens of a heaven-sent opportunity.

Later in the day the real estate representative called me to tell me that the $1,500 (which I hoped was still available) would not be enough; that another $1,000 was needed to cover the minimum down payment. The additional sum seemed preposterous and impossible to secure, but we were very fortunate in being able to borrow it from a friend, who was most gracious. We were delighted with our new site and anticipated moving our "family" there the next September, by which time I calculated that I could repay a large portion of the borrowed money.

Not many months before the somewhat hectic move to our country estate, the family of my very first patient came to visit her. We had become close friends with her two brothers and a sister during her years in my care, and we enjoyed their company often. I invited one of the brothers to visit the new place we'd described so vividly on previous occasions, and I described my long-range plans as we toured the grounds. Not knowing that he was to be our benefactor in the near future, I divulged all the financial problems I expected to encounter as our plans slowly progressed. Much to my joy, he said, "I have a little money to back you, so you go ahead and draw your plans for exactly what you want and need." I could hardly believe my ears.

A week later the brother returned with the president of a local bank; they looked around briefly and almost silently, then said, "Good-bye" — nothing more. As my husband and I pondered the outcome of their visit, we feared again that our credit rating would be the downfall; our pasts were not entirely an asset. We realized, too, that should the loan be granted, paying the interest and buying the furnishings while continuing to operate would be a financial strain. With so much in the balance, we relaxed and put the problem in God's hands.

A few days later we gathered in the attorney's office to close the transaction, and upon the receipt of $33,000 I nearly fainted. In all my years I don't believe I have ever experienced such a sensation. We were both overwhelmed, and very grateful. I never believed anyone had that much money; let alone willing to let us borrow it.

XII

MY ANSWER TO PRAYER

The much dreamed of and most careful plans for the wing to be added to our nursing home to the specification of State requirements were ideal, and the building was destined to become a model. Aspiring to such a large and efficient building, our funds diminished rapidly. With contractors of all sorts being paid, materials and supplies to buy, fixtures and appliances to install, we feared that we neared a danger point as the building neared completion. Another State requirement was maintaining adequate operating capital, and the approaching depletion was alarming.

One afternoon as I watched the building progress, I didn't recognize an old model car coming up the winding drive. The automobile was so old that I couldn't detect the manufacturer on first sight, but I soon recognized the driver as my wonderful, generous and devoted husband. He had taken his brand new Oldsmobile downtown and sold it. In that dilapidated old Chevrolet he returned with money in his pocket to put toward operating costs.

There was a lot of good use available yet from the little old car, as it shuttled laundry, groceries and supplies back and forth on numerous daily trips to town. When the doors finally fell off, it was no longer useful, even for hauling leaves on yard-cleaning day.

Our demanding routine required long hours of diligence, but together we enjoyed a quiet pride in our accomplishments. Our lives were filled with joy and satisfaction supreme as we watched our prayers answered. Silken strings, beautiful and secure with faith, hope and love were woven into our daily lives, which we dedicated to our nursing home for the aged.

Dedication Day in 1958 found our nursing home jumping with activity. With flowers, messages of congratulations and best wishes; doctors, ministers, friends and families of the patients, and friends and families of our own on the scene, it was a joyous day for us all. We had moved five patients to the new quarters, and two new ones had joined the group the same week. With guidance and strength from God, we had come a long way. We are equipped to care for twenty-five guests at the present.

I couldn't begin to describe each and every dear patient, as each one and I share a special feeling or respect. We try hard to make this home as much like their own as possible, so they may be happy and comfortable.

On opening the new home, a very prominent railroad executive, his mother being among the first new patients admitted, gave us our slogan one day as we considered what to print on the stationery and cards — "A Home with a Heart". The staff and I try to work and live by the slogan and the result is evident in the cheery atmosphere throughout. The same gentleman may have sensed our strained financial status in that we lacked a few essentials on opening day. When his mother passed away several months later, he made a sizeable cash donation in her memory, with which we were able to install a chain-link fence around the grounds, making for greater safety as the more active patients visit outdoors among the flowers and plants, many of which have been given by families who have lost their loved ones. Clothing objects and items of all sorts have often been left for someone not so materially fortunate to use. There is a lovely plaque on the main door placed by a family in memory of their loved one. Little can all the generous friends realize the important part they play in making this house a home and haven.

Some of our guests are more sensitive or confused than others, and as they are free to mingle when physically able, petty differences arise occasionally, but with a little T. L. C. (Tender Loving Care) the disagreement can be amicably settled and forgotten. Gentle persuasion is quite often necessary, but everyone works together toward the best interests of all.

It is rather nostalgic to listen to stories from the past, sometimes related by a memory eighty or more years old, recalling life on the farm when everything was scheduled around milking-time. To one, a memory is so vivid that he may try to leave the house to feed the chickens, but with a little gentleness, he is returned to the present. To another, a buggy-ride down the main thoroughfare before dark highlights his recollections, and it certainly would be romantic, wouldn't it? Reminiscing can be fun.

Many of our guests are with us by choice, and many for various and differing reasons. None were sent for the lack of family love or compassion, but many situations are best solved in soliciting our assistance. Most of our patients have grown children, some of whom are employed away from their homes, while other patients may have grandchildren with whom tensions naturally arise. Elderly persons can't, and shouldn't, be left alone, relegated to a lonely, miserable later life, and I am happy that our facilities offer companionship with their contemporaries, as well as afford the best of physical care.

Among the hardest things I had to learn to accept was the inevitable loss of a friend and patient whom God called away. After such close association, the sadness is almost more than I could bear, but as the families of the departed return for an occasional visit, I am comforted.

Since our beginning, we have been fortunate to have the services of three wonderful physicians, who stand ready to come on a moment's notice; and cordially answer my calls for information, day or night. I long ago revealed to them my alcoholic weakness, and I am sure it was a prescription straight from their hearts when they counselled and encouraged me during the few times of darkness or despondency within the past several years. I have appreciated their personal assistance to me as well as their capable services to our patients.

Our registered nurse, Gwen Bull, shares efficiently in the love and understanding that abounds in our home, making her daily rounds as supervisor a welcomed routine for the past four years. She is a small brunette with a gentle smile, and well able to cope with the demands. Subjected to night calls, she remains ever ready with her medical assistance to her patients and our guests, but she has also been a willing listener to my problems. Though she knew very little about an alcoholic's emotional disturbances when she came to work, she has learned much by attending A.A. meetings with Ford and me, and even made a "Twelfth Step" call with us to visit an A.A. member who suffered a relapse recently. As an energetic and sympathetic young person, we feel blessed in having her services and friendship.

I've not stopped dreaming, for my plans for the future include enlarging the building to accommodate many more ladies and gentlemen. The waiting list grows steadily. I have confidence that my prayer for this endeavor will be answered, too, someday; but meanwhile, I pray for guidance and strength to meet the challenge of the day.

Yes, there was found at last a place for me in this huge, busy world, and I just wish it hadn't taken me so long to find it. With the continued help of God we're climbing toward the top of a mountain, and though I rarely wonder if we shall ever reach the crest, I realize there is enrichment in trying. God had a master plan when He made our lovely nursing home a reality, and with Him we want to share it with others. Besides, in our efforts I have lost a most powerful enemy.

Among the first visitors to our new building was a State employee. After showing him around the building, we returned to my office for a cup of coffee and a friendly chat, though at first I dreaded the possibility that in some way we may not have met the rigid State requirements. The gentleman asked, "By the way, do you know Miss So-and-So? She asked to be remembered to you."

Catching breaths of fear, I wondered if I should admit to remembering a ghost from my past, as such would inevitably occur, and I associated the vaguely familiar name with a sordid incident. I nodded, "Yes, I know her slightly, though after all these years I should think she would have forgotten me."

I remembered her well as the administrator of the

little hospital to which I had been admitted on the verge of an alcoholic's death over three years previous. Frightened and ashamed to discuss the circumstances surrounding our mutual acquaintance, I wasn't sure I wanted this stranger from the State office to learn of my past. But perhaps the administrator of the little hospital had already informed him. Should that be the case, I decided there was little I could do but admit the truth. I hoped that the State employee would understand that my past was all water under the bridge, as I smiled faintly, and with a silent prayer deep in my heart, I disclosed the nature of my visit to that particular hospital. Then I explained that it was during that confinement that God and I became true partners, and I then began to make steady progress toward real recovery.

After my honest confession, we continued our visit to become close, understanding friends; for it developed that a dear friend of his suffered with my old problem, and I tried to suggest in my simple way, a few measures with which to tackle the disease. I explained my own recovery plan, and the need to first become genuinely sincere and intent. Without that will, the disease is incurable. I hoped that I could be an example to his friend by casting a ray of light and a spirit of hope in his direction. Thereafter, I no longer shook in my boots when a State employee came on the premises, for in them I found much needed advice and instruction.

As a famous philosopher wrote, "We have to lose ourselves in order to find ourselves", it befits an alcoholic to understand that it was all to easy to lose himself, but he must expect many difficulties in finding himself a useful human being again. The route of alcoholism is a tragic road leading down, down and further down, winding endlessly to nothing. Unless the suffering traveler really wants to turn back and tread uphill, he is the victim of rugged detours. Once obtaining the real, true stamina, he should realize that he cannot make his return to sobriety alone — for the trip requires many helping, understanding friends; and strength from God. With confidence in himself, reliance upon God and help from others, a safe return is assured, but a slow day by day challenge must be anticipated.

While visiting with Mom and accompanying her to church, I often found it difficult to restrain myself from fingering the keys at the organ. The impluse was almost childish, but my love for music has materialized. I now have an organ of my own, which is a source of real joy to me and to all the guests as well. Always on Sunday and as often during the week as there is time, we enjoy gathering together in the front room to sing favorite songs; it is I who accompanies the failing, though eager, old voices. Each Sunday evening we are fortunate to have a minister from one of the several participating Protestant Churches come into our home to hold a devotional service, which is followed by singing and fellowship. The visiting pastors encourage the patients and me as well, as we work and live each day, a day at a time.

With my self-respect restored, and nurturing my God-given talents with personal pride, I have regained the love of my family. They look forward to seeing me, and we visit on their porch openly and to the approval of the neighbors, from whom my family had suffered scorn on my account. Shirley lives with me and we enjoy being together; in fact, as bookkeeper and a week-end helper, she is much needed and appreciated.

My beloved Mom Turpin has flown from Los Angeles twice for extended visits with me, the most recent of which, at seventy-two years of age, was made even more memorable when she chose a jet flight. I'm sure many of Mom's charges have made a successful return to sobriety, but none can cherish Mom any dearer than I.

Old and new friends call often, both by phone and in person, and our week-ends have a joyful, holiday atmosphere as we welcome them. Rid of all those old, hard feelings of resentment and distrust, I enjoy companionship with each and every one. Even though I run the risk of repetition, I want to emphasize my complete, happy freedom from the influence of alcohol, and quote our nurse, Gwen Bull in this respect:

"You can have everything you want in life — or you can have nothing."

Now that I have regained all that I lost during those wasted years, an even closer inspection shows that I have everything.

I am not afraid of the Dusk any more, or the revealing sunshine that comes with the Dawning. With God's ever watchful eye over me, I sleep in peace.

THE END